Louis Nowra was born in Melbourne.
He is a playwright, novelist, and
screenwriter. He lives in Sydney.

BRIEF LIVES is a series of short, personal books
about well-known people and their work. Other titles
include *The War Letters of General Monash* and *Side by
Side*, Sebastian Smee's book on Matisse and Picasso.

WARNE'S WORLD

WARNE'S WORLD

Louis Nowra

Duffy & Snellgrove
Sydney

Published by Duffy & Snellgrove in 2002
PO Box 177 Potts Point NSW 1335 Australia
info@duffyandsnellgrove.com.au

Distributed by Pan Macmillan

© Amanita Pty. Ltd. 2002

Cover design by Alex Snellgrove
Cover image by Newspix
Typeset by Cooper Graphics
Printed by Griffin Press

ISBN 1 876631 53 8

visit our website: www.duffyandsnellgrove.com.au

Author's Note

This is a book for cricket lovers and those who have an interest in Shane Warne or would like to know what all the fuss is about. I have tried to keep statistics to a minimum. For those who want to read about the more arcane and esoteric statistics regarding Warne's career, I recommend *The Complete Shane Warne* by Ken Piesse. Although there is a bibliography at the rear of this book, it is obvious that I have relied for many facts on *Shane Warne, My Autobiography* and *Bold Warnie* by Roland Perry. I have also gone through countless newspaper reports about Warne. They are so voluminous that the stuff written about him seems more than anyone could read in a lifetime. What did surprise me was just how sanctimonious, pompous and moralistic some journalists can be, although many more were astute and had interesting interpretations of Warne, some of which I have incorporated. The cricket reporter whom I seldom quote but who was unfailing interesting, both in his observations and language, was Peter Roebuck. His style may occasionally verge on an idiosyncratic blend of Neville Cardus and camp and he was always wonderfully readable. I must also thank Michelle Bentley for her last-minute research.

Louis Nowra, Kings Cross
August 2002

To Mandy

Contents

Introduction

It always seems to be hot. The heat is dry, almost air-less and scorching out of the shade. My kelpie lies on his stomach in the shadows of the eastern section of our housing commission house which is baking in the sun and he watches me hammer, with the end of my bat handle, three pieces of a broomstick into the hard earth at the far end of the backyard. Although the bat is made of inexpensive willow and will never hit a real leather cricket ball, I have lovingly rubbed it with paraffin oil for the required two weeks as instructed by a boy at school. The rubber casing on the handle is firm and black but having been through several similar bats I know that by the time summer is over the cheap rubber will be frayed and motley and through the ragged holes I will see the tightly wound red stitching underneath.

By now my kelpie is alert (his demented enthusiasm the product of his previous owner, a mad, cruel farmer) because the triptych of sticks means that a game is about to take place. He watches me intensely as I impatiently bounce a tennis ball – shaved on one side to help it swing – on the full blade of my bat as I wait for my opponent, the only boy in a street filled with girls (this ratio the byproduct, some people say, of the quality of our water supply).

The pitch stretches from the backdoor steps to just inside the rear fence. The poor volcanic soil is cracked and covered in a thin sheen of dried and dead grass that shines in the bright sunlight. Halfway across the pitch there are two stunted silhouettes of the clothes lines which are tied to two crossbars resembling crucifixes that in turn are attached to two posts planted on the eastern and western sides of the yard. What my mate doesn't realise – and never will – is that I have placed the stumps in such a position that a right-handed batsman will have a large crack in the earth on a good length in front of his off stump. If a ball ever hits the crack it will behave in a disturbingly unpredictable fashion.

My dog's ears prick up a few moments before the backyard gate squeaks open and rattles shut and he scurries from the shade into the glare and enthusiastically jumps on Peter, eager for the match to begin. Depending on the toss of a coin or even the bat, I will be representing Australia or, if unlucky, the Poms. Next are the arguments; do we have the leg before wicket rule? This is contentious. Because he protects his wicket with his legs Peter is rarely bowled, except for the occasional shooter when the ball hits the crack and skids through his defences. Even though I know he's right and that it's unfair for the bowler to decide whether the batsman is out leg before I argue vehemently for it, eventually trading off my acquiescence for my wish that my dog act as a fieldsman. This is a touchy subject. I demand that Smokey's catches mean you're out but the trouble is that my dog seems to take a higher percentage of catches off my bowling than Peter's. Then, of course, there is the fact that as the day wears on the ball becomes slippery and gruesome with canine saliva, but even though Peter will grimace picking up the saliva-soaked ball dropped at his feet by the panting kelpie he realises that in the oppressive heat it's probably better that Smokey does all the fielding.

So through the long hot day we emulate our cricket heroes, pretending to be the handsome leg spinner Richie Benaud, the thuggish English fast bowler Freddie Trueman or, for Peter, the right-handed batsman, Norm O'Neill, or in my case, in an era that seemed denuded of left-handers, the thrilling all-rounder, Alan Davidson. We don't quite know what the words mean but we pretend we're going to bowl a Chinaman or a leg cutter. Peter curses when an acrobatic Smokey jumps up into the air to snaffle a catch from a wild smash. There is an argument about whether a ball caught from a ricochet off the house is really a catch or not, and there is a surreptitious creep into the yard of the neighbour on the left, who has threatened to keep our ball if we continue to jump over the fence and land in his precious flower garden. We don't worry about the house on the right because every weekday, while her husband is at work, the next-door neighbour retires to her bedroom with a man who arrives on the dot at midday. The only time we see her is when the ball bounces against her bedroom window or even breaks it, but by the time she is peering through the shattered glass our backyard is empty and the culprits are lying in the shade of the eastern side of the house, feeling slightly guilty – even the dog seems guilty – but miffed that we have lost a ball and are unable to continue the game.

If there are no lost balls or broken windows the game continues until sunset, the appeals just as ferocious (it is forgotten that we decided not to have the leg before rule), the ball so soggy that when you hit it a spray of Smokey's saliva veils your face in a moist mist, the limbs weary, the dog snatching quick respites in the shade in between innings. As the western crucifix shadow remorselessly creeps across the pitch we know I will soon be hearing my mother at the back door calling me to wash up for tea, and Peter will trudge back through the still stifling heat to his home where he, like I, will regale those at the dinner table with tales of astounding feats. In these stories my leg spinner will be spun with truly mythic diagonal turn and my cover drive will be transformed from clumsy sketch to an immaculate oil painting.

These cricket matches continued until one day I returned outside from the kitchen after having had a glass of water only to see Peter running from the backyard, blood streaming from his head. I asked him what had happened but he was too distraught to reply and fled back to his place. My pale-faced sister was standing nearby with the blood-stained cricket bat in her hand and said she had hit my friend on the head. When I asked why, she sniffled and said: 'Because I love him.'

Cricket was no match for the impenetrable logic of female love.

The cricket wasn't over when summer waned because in winter there was a chance that Australia would be playing the Poms in England. The Melbourne cold had me snuggled up in bed and I'd lie under the bedclothes, transistor earplug safely nuzzled in my left ear, and listen to those calm, measured voices describing the Ashes matches in such reverent tones that a Test at Lord's seemed more a description of a church service than a sporting event and the deeds of both sides more heroic, more august than what happened in Australia, except for the puzzling fact that English summers, interrupted by rain and low temperatures, were more like the Melbourne winter I was enduring. Then, having unknowingly drifted off to sleep during the night, I would wake up to discover that the batteries of my transistor had wasted away and that if I wanted to hear the next night's broadcast I had to go bottle collecting to earn money to buy new ones.

Cricket and football were the two most important things of my childhood and teenage years, but the short, athletic, sometimes brutal Australian Rules games had none of the majestic slowness and subtle inflections of Test cricket where, much to the astonishment of those who know nothing of the game, it can continue for five days and not have a result yet still prove extraordinarily exciting. I remember the tie between the West Indies and Australia, of which I avidly listened to on our kitchen radio propped up on top of the refrigerator as my bemused mother attempted to prepare tea, having to push me away from the refrigerator door every time she needed something, so oblivious and enthralled was I by the nail-biting finish after five exhilarating days of fever-ishly imagining the game through the voices of the commentators.

When we shifted from my working-class suburb to a middle-class one and a house next to a mental asylum, the front yard had a long concrete driveway. If I couldn't play with the policeman's sons a few doors down I spent all day bowling uphill on the driveway, which finished abruptly at a wooden fence, its palings stained a rusty colour. Now that Smokey was dead it was up to me to fetch the ball, and if the tennis ball hit the centre of a paling it would slowly return down the con-crete path to me, but if it nicked an overlapping join then it would jump off at erratic angles. I had marked three stumps on the fence and for hour after hour through the hot days (and it seemed that there were no rainy days when playing cricket in an Australian summer) I'd bowl to imaginary English batsmen. Because of the short run-up I was reduced to bowling spinners even though my temperament was decidedly that of a fast bowler. I was generally triumphant against the Poms, cunningly floating the tennis ball through the hot thin air so it dropped unexpectedly on them and turned viciously on the glaring hot concrete, leaving the bewildered batsman stranded between defence and attack, between befuddlement and awe, the ball either nicking the side of the bat, when the paling fence would magically metamorphose into a wicket-keeper or first slip who took the catch, or it clipping the off stump, or, once I had perfected my wrong'un or googly, turning the opposite way to what was expected and darting through the clumsy defence of the surprised Pommie batsman to take the middle stump. If Test cricket were being played in Australia then the transistor was at the bowler's end so I could mimic the events unfolding in Brisbane or Sydney or Adelaide. I never felt lonely bowling all afternoon but deliciously contented, as if in the rhythm of bowling and fetching I had obtained the nirvana of having achieved in my imagination the dream of becoming a Test cricketer.

But of course I never did achieve it in reality. I went from school cricket to Saturday cricket played on matting or, if lucky, a turf wicket. By the time I went to university and afterwards I found the attractions of theatre, drugs and sex had undermined my interest in cricket, but during the late 1970s my interest was rekindled by the lethal pace combination of Lillee and Thomson who brutally dominated the English and West Indians. Even on television the chant of *Lillee, Lillee* as the bowler came in had an intimidatory feel, not unlike, I imagine, blood-thirsty Roman crowds in a coliseum cheering an armed gladiator relentlessly moving in on a solitary, hapless Christian. His lithe, almost graceful run to the wicket was undercut by his bristling moustache, a headband trying to keep the last of his unruly hair in place and a permanent scowl that indicated a hatred of batsmen so profound that I am sure that some mentally buckled before the ball reached them.

During the 1980s I played Sunday social cricket,

mainly for a team captained by the playwright Alex
Buzo. And here I should mention how playwrights have
had an especial love of the game. Way back in 1873
Garnet Walch wrote *Australia Felix*, a play about the
activities of various diabolical beings who are determined to spread discord and misery through Australia
during the visit of the English cricketers under the leadership of the great W.G. Grace with a subplot consisting
of the eponymous Felix gaining and losing a magic bat
that would ensure an Australian victory. There are also
playwrights such as Samuel Beckett, apparently handy
enough to play first-class cricket for Ireland, Tom Stoppard, whose play *The Real Thing* contains a delightful
speech about cricket, Alan Ayckbourn, and Harold
Pinter whose lines 'They were watering the wicket at
Melbourne' came out in the German translation as
'They were pissing on the wicket fence in Melbourne'
and who also wrote the screenplays for the films *Accident*
and *The Go-Between*, which feature cricket matches that
carry huge symbolic weight. I led the bowling averages
and incurred a visit to Balmain hospital after being hit
in the cheek when opening the batting, the result of
which was a fetching scar. In his book *Glancing Blows*
Buzo referred to me as 'The Mean Machine' and called
me 'very competitive and temperamental', the latter epi-
thet unfortunately deserved. Once I threw my bat away
on leaving the oval after an extremely dubious leg
before decision and it nearly hit his astonished daughter,
who was amazed at how such a violent reaction could
erupt from such a seemingly placid game.

In Tests Australia's fortunes had changed and now it

was the West Indies team that dominated cricket mainly due to its pace attack, especially the quartet of the sombre Andy Roberts, Colin Croft, Joel Garner and Michael Holding. The fearsome foursome helped make the teams led by Clive Lloyd and then Viv Richards the greatest in Test cricket. These fast bowlers were the most savage and relentless in the history of the game. After one duo finished the other two would take over so that the batsmen had no respite. Even if your courage didn't falter, the sheer relentless barrage would inflict severe physical damage and wear down your concentration. If that weren't enough, the batsmen found it hard to score quickly because with the bowlers' long run-ups and languid manner in between deliveries it meant there were less balls bowled. By the end of the 1980s, it was not only that the dominance of the West Indian attack was proving tiresome, the slow over rates and lack of variation were proving as boring as the sluggish scoring of the 1950s before Richie Benaud became captain and, with the West Indies captain Frank Worrell, reinvigorated a game gone stale.

The few Test matches I went to see during the late 1980s and early 1990s were dull. If the West Indians were bowling then one prepared oneself for countless bouncers and the sight of batsmen doubling over after being hit by a ball hurled at them at around 150 kilometres an hour. There might be one or two gritty and defiant innings and a cavalier knock that owed much to a good eye and luck but really it was like watching a surfeit of car crashes. None of the bowlers had much interest for me except for Michael Holding, whose run-up was so graceful, so quiet, so unassuming that it made him seem to glide over the ground more like a hovercraft than a clumsy ferry cutting through waves, and it was no wonder that some batsmen were mesmerised and had to remind themselves, many times too late, that he was delivering a leather ball at a pace that could kill.

One day in Adelaide I went to see Australia play Pakistan because I wanted to see Abdul Qadir, a leg spinner of whom I had heard so much. Now the game was different. The rhythm and pace of it seemed simultaneously to slow down and quicken. Like all spinners, he went through his over in a quarter of the time of the West Indian quick bowlers and instead of the brutal logic of fast bowling, Qadir's every ball was fraught with ambiguity. Would it drop suddenly on the batsman? Would it hurry through? Would it spin the opposite way to what the batsman expected? Would the tempting ball tossed high into the air really be as innocuous as it looked? Now cricket took on another aspect. Instead of relying on their reflexes as they did against the fast bowlers, the batsmen had to wait, and to think, and to worry, and know that the possibilities of what the spinning ball could do seemed infinite when bowled by the gifted Qadir. He didn't take many wickets that day but I returned home that night mentally exhausted from watching him. I remember the appreciative silence that went around the crowd when he came on to bowl – he was a bowler who mentally threatened you and who played tricks with your mind.

There were some other leg-spinners of interest but

then along came the roly-poly Shane Warne. His début was one of the most inauspicious for some time. Where Qadir's run-up was bouncy with a high-spirited jump near the end and, at the point of delivery, a windmill spin of arms as he let the ball go, Warne seemed to plod in for a few flat-footed steps and, with a grunt of great physical effort, deliver the ball. Yet, although his style was not as exuberant or impressive as the Pakistani's, Warne was to transform cricket. It didn't happen easily. His first few Tests were a bewildering mixture of the occasional success subverted by a series of inconsequential performances. But by 1993, when he bowled what was quickly termed 'the ball of the century', he had become one of the most exciting cricketers of our time. Not only did he come along when the game was stagnating under the monotonous diet of fast bowling but his success, his prodigious ability and showmanship enticed people back to watching Test cricket. Even now when he comes on to bowl people stop talking in a hotel or while listening to the radio description or at the game. He may not be the talent he was, but he is still a master of spin, a bowler of great guile and supreme con artist and every ball he bowls potentially threatens the batsman. It was noticeable at the last day of the Third Test against South Africa in Sydney in early 2002 that the brilliant fast bowler Glenn McGrath was accorded a blasé reception from the spectators, but when Warne came on to bowl the crowd fell silent and held its breath as each ball looped and spun through the air. After each delivery all heads turned towards the replay screen and a collective *Oh!* or *Ah!* escaped as the slow-motion replay showed just how much the ball had spun or how tantalisingly close it came to nicking the edge of the bat. Some consider him past his best, but every time critics or fans write him off, he comes back. He was once admired and even adored but after all the scandals and controversies there is now an ambiguous attitude to him even in Australia. However there is no mistaking that he is one of the finest bowlers in the history of the game and he has personally saved Test cricket when it was in danger of ossifying and dying out.

Since the first ball Shane Warne bowled in Test cricket to the present day as he approaches the twilight of his career, he has given me immense pleasure, made me admire his cricketing greatness and occasionally made me gasp at his indiscretions. This is less a biography than a wide-ranging appreciation of Warne's supreme gifts as a cricketer. It takes in his follies, his boofhead behaviour, the scandals, the influence of television in making him so popular, how he changed Test cricket, the way the public has loved and reviled him and the way he has been shaped by our national identity. It is also an appreciation of a man whose talent can sometimes approach the sublime beauty of a piece of music or poetry.

1 : The Man

Probably one of the most famous cricketers of all time and voted one of the five greatest cricketers of the twentieth century by *Wisden*, the so-called cricket bible, Shane Warne is one of the best-paid and wealthiest sportsmen in Australia. Yet, if you did not know him and saw him walking down a suburban street you might glance at him and, quickly taking in his plump figure, sun-blasted face, earring and bottle-blond hair, think he was merely a superannuated surfie. His face is a cartoonist's nightmare because it contains no sharp lines and, perhaps, only a child attempting to draw it by mangling a square, rectangle and an oval could catch its likeness. The lips have been made taut and tight by the combination of zinc cream and sun, and his pale green eyes are like shelled pistachio nuts sinking into a bowl of blancmange. His hands are huge and his fingers are like enormous, plump Havana cigars. His arms and wrists would suit a wood chopper. And then there is his physique. In these days of trim sports bodies tensely sculpted and defined in a gym, his ranges between the fat and the merely chubby. Yet this man, who when he played his first Test match resembled more a pudgy barfly coming on to bowl in a Sunday park match between two pub cricket teams than an élite cricketer, has transformed Test cricket, become the second-highest wicket-taker of all time, made opposing teams bat first rather than face him on the final day when cricket pitches suit his bowling, and even forced groundsmen to tamper with a cricket pitch to try to nullify his bowling. He has mentally demolished some batsmen so completely that they have had to seek help from psychiatrists. He has become a household name in every cricketing nation. As David Hopps, an English writer, commented: 'Aw, c'mon, everyone knows about Warnie: the reformed surfie [*sic*], the jewellery, the blond highlights, the endless magazine shoots, the weight problem, the rumours about the chronic shoulder and finger injuries. Oh, yes, and the leggie, the googly, the flipper, the top-spinner, the zooter, the latest mystery ball …' Or as an Australian journalist wrote: 'Warne is Australia's most recognisable and roguish character.'

At times even some of his fellow players seem in awe of him, calling him 'a magician', 'our blond superstar', 'genius' and 'The Showman'. In the early days of his fame he was photographed as a magician pulling cricket balls out of a top hat. For many spectators he *was* a magician and it seemed very few batsmen could read him, and every ball seemed an act of inexplicable sorcery. He bewitched batsmen so much that they took to examining slow-motion and close-up television replays just so they could try to understand how his wrist and fingers were able to conjure up such a disturbing variety of different deliveries. Perhaps it's simpler and more Australian to say that at his peak Warne dazzled batsmen so much it was as if they were kangaroos caught in the spotlight of a particularly aggressive and brilliant roo shooter.

Yet there are other sides to Warne. Some people and commentators regard him as 'a lair', 'snake-oil salesman' or a 'yob'. To his former Captain, Allan Border, he is 'a knockabout bloke' and to Warne's team-mates like Justin Langer, he is 'our lovable rogue'. Many fellow players and the occasional journalist have commented on his uncomplicated charm but also his larrikin impulses, whether it be giving the finger to a crowd, celebrating victory by gyrating wildly with a stump on the balcony of a cricket dressing-room, poking out his ample stomach or publicly scoffing from a champagne bottle in front of English spectators as if he were in a pub with a couple of mates. In today's sports world where image is becoming increasingly important, these acts are not seen as joyous outbursts of a simple bloke by Australian cricket authorities and writers but as behaviour reeking of poor taste. To use the cliché, it is 'simply not cricket'.

Possessed of a certain childlike *naïveté* off the cricket paddock he is frequently puzzled or annoyed at how this sort of behaviour or aspects of his private life have become the microscopic focus of the media. When his indiscretions are discovered his reaction is generally the same. There is the slightly guilty look of a schoolboy found smoking behind the shelter shed (almost literally in one infamous case) and a defence that seems to say that the sin wasn't a mistake – only been found out was. In a way his defence is that of Bart Simpson – I didn't do it, you didn't see me do it.

For a man who has a deep desire to be liked, Warne has always found official attempts to tame him hard to fathom. In the beginning of his career he was unconditionally loved, but after the scandalous revelations of the past few years he seems genuinely upset that some people now revile him. He is not a deep thinker. For him God is 'the Bloke Upstairs' and his philosophy of life is simple: 'I am pretty straightforward, I don't talk behind people's backs. If I have a problem with someone, I confront them. I don't like dwelling on things. I move on. The sun comes up in the morning and I have a smile on my dial.' When he has been pushed to try to explain anything deeper all he can come up with is: 'Take the good with the bad, that's what life is about.' His lack of curiosity about politics, the countries he tours or art and literature is a congenital characteristic. He seems to have never read a book. He might flip through one of the many books his captain, Steve Waugh, has made out of his tour diaries, but he only looks at the pictures. The only book he has been pictured sneaking a glance at is his ghosted autobiography, leading to speculation that he may never have read even it. The only magazine ever pictured in his hand is one about motor vehicles, which is logical given his fondness for sports cars – he has been the proud owner of a red Ferrari. Now, given the growing size of his family, he drives a black Mercedes sedan. His music tastes are simple, basically rock-and-roll bands like U2 and Bon Jovi.

His success is often remarked on but what is seldom recognised is his courage. Time and time again he has come back from shoulder and finger injuries that would have destroyed a lesser cricketer. If Bill Clinton was the Comeback Kid in American politics, Warne is the Comeback Kid of cricket. Many times, especially recently, he has been all but dismissed as a has-been, only to prove at crucial times that he is, in the true sense of the word, a champion. It is sometimes forgotten that his courage and perseverance are quite formidable even under the most trying conditions.

Warne's fame has come at a personal cost. He is more guarded than when he started out and at times is justifiably suspicious of print journalists, although not so much of television reporters, because he can control his image on television. When he has to confess his sins it is always to a pliable and sympathetic television reporter. He is attracted to television, partly because he knows the medium, having worked in it himself, but also because he knows that it will always be sympathetic to him because he attracts huge viewing audiences when he is playing. He and the media have worked symbiotically to create the Warne myth. It's probably good that he has the television media on side, because the scandals he has been associated with mean that it's easier to give his side of the story more directly on television than to a newspaper journalist who might interpret, and, to his eyes, distort what he was attempting to say.

Increasingly Warne's cricketing career has been

dogged and sometimes overshadowed by scandal and headlines, whether it be betting and corruption, sexual peccadilloes, controversies on the field or extortion attempts. He is right when he says that his life has been a soap opera. The primary effect of all these incidents has been to thwart his major ambition, which is to captain Australia. But all through his successes, tribulations, stupidities and controversies nothing can undermine the fact that he has proved to be the most exciting and charismatic cricketer of his generation. Don Bradman, seldom given to hyperbole, called Warne 'the best thing that's happened to the game for many, many years'.

In the film *Amadeus* the envious and bland composer Salieri is astonished by Mozart's ineffable music but can't fathom how someone who is so childish, simple, delighted by scatology and sex, and incapable of articulating his own genius, should be the possessor of such a gift. It is as if God is channelling music through the simple human container that is Mozart. In a similar way one can look at Warne and ask oneself — how did a boofhead like him achieve such a rare and wondrous ability? Terry Jenner, Warne's mentor, quite simply sums up his rare talent as 'a gift from God'.

2: The Gift

Warne may have a gift from God but a spinner, especially a leg spinner, is in league with the Devil. Part of his skill is based on trickery, chicanery and deceit. Like a grand chess master a leg spinner must think several moves ahead, he must make the batsmen wrongly second-guess him or even mentally resign in complete bewilderment. Leg spin bowling is the most arcane and esoteric of all of cricket's many skills. It requires mental courage, practised expertise and simple rat-cunning. The master leg spinner is equivalent of the riverboat gambler with aces up his sleeve, the pool hall hustler, the stage magician, and even the shyster planning the three-shell trick. And in all these things the result is similar; there is the gasping admiration of the spectators, but for the victim himself there is a sense of diminishment, knowing full well he has been deceived but not knowing how.

For people following Warne's career his genius has also provided a sense of pure aesthetic satisfaction, as if he had transcended the ordinary prose of most cricket and given it a poetical richness, whose pleasures even countless video replays of his most marvellous wicket-taking deliveries cannot dim. Not only is it a continuing delight to review those special deliveries, it is a treat to see the reactions of the batsmen: the disbelieving Gatting having been bowled by the so-called 'ball of the century', the normally condescending Richie Richardson stunned at the astounding ball that has just taken his wicket, or Shivnarine Chanderpaul, who had been batting with supreme confidence, almost reeling backwards, amazed by how a ball could have spun a metre and hit his stumps.

Like many cricketers, or for that matter great actors or mathematicians, Warne cannot explain his gift or even articulate it in an interesting manner. It is as if he is a conduit for it, just as a great opera singer seems a medium for his or her special talent. But it is important to consider just what this gift entails and why it is so extraordinary, in order to see why Shane Warne is so special.

Leg spin bowling is a precious and complex art. And it is an unnatural and rare gift, or as Brian Wilkins puts it in *Cricket: The Bowler's Art*, 'Like the giant pandas carted around the zoos and stared at by millions, leg spin bowlers – also an endangered species – attract attention which is inversely proportional to their numbers.' Although one can learn the rudiments of the craft, it takes a special talent to master it. Much of its subtlety is passed from mouth to mouth because when leg spinners come to write their memoirs, they still cannot refrain from loquacious deceit and deliberate obfuscation, and they seldom publicly pass on the actual mechanics of how they spun the ball and what individual tricks they used. It could be said that like stage magicians they want to carry the secret of their legerdemain to their graves.

In order to appreciate this art it is necessary to describe its genesis. In the early days of cricket when the ball was bowled underarm, the natural method of spinning the ball was from right to left or in cricket parlance from the leg stump to the off stump. That is, the ball was directed towards the right-handed batsman's legs, his leg stump, and then would spin away from his legs towards the off side or off stump. It was much more difficult to spin the ball from off stump to leg. The opposite problem happened when cricketers started to bowl overarm. The natural way to throw a ball is not unlike throwing a javelin, so that the ball, having been thrown, goes straight. When it bounces, the natural shoulder action or easy twist of the wrist makes the ball deviate from left to right. Bowling over the shoulder (overarm) leg spin the rotation is anti-clockwise and the effort to rotate the ball places tremendous pressure on the shoulder and the wrist. One just has to examine Warne's thick wrists to realise they have a natural and resilient torsion, while his massive fingers can impart considerable spin. As his mentor Terry Jenner has remarked: 'He has fabulous hand strength but the curious thing is that he doesn't get a mark on his spinning fingers. He never has any calluses because of his strong wrist.' Richie Benaud has summed up the skill: 'Bowling leg spin is a very difficult business. It's hard on the fingers, tendons and shoulder and the brain as well.' Because this is such a difficult art one of the first and most frustrating things a tyro leg spinner has to learn is control. In fact over the years it has been considered that a leg spinner, because of his potential for inaccuracy, costs his own side many runs in order to gain a wicket. As Benaud has said of a leg spinner: 'He distributes his gifts like a millionaire.' However, Warne hates to bowl in that cavalier style and is a determinedly frugal bowler. His accuracy is astonishing and atypical. He has little time for the idea that leg spinners are profligate, even though leg spinner Arthur Mailey once said of his own bowling: 'Sometimes I am attacked by waves of accuracy and I don't trust them.' Warne has none of the genial temperament of Mailey, and attacks the batsmen with the urgent vehemence of a fast bowler not unlike the great Australian leg spinner Bill O'Reilly whose eyes would blaze with hatred for the batsmen and whose delivery stride was a windmill swirl of arms as if he were caught up in the angry breeze of his contempt for them. Even bowling against a fellow team-mate Warne cannot restrain himself and once, during a net session, thoroughly enjoyed reducing a Victorian Sheffield Shield colleague to tears of embarrassment and frustration.

The essential movement of the leg spinner is one where you hold your arm erect, with the back of your hand pointing towards the sky, turning your hand anti-clockwise as you bowl. What comes into play is how far the ball spins, how far it drifts in the air, whether it is of a low or high trajectory and how fast it is bowled. The spin imparted and the precise moment it has left the hand mean that even a ball that doesn't bounce before it reaches the batsman can drop alarmingly, as if flouting the laws of aerodynamics.

At the end of the nineteenth century there originated a radical new delivery, a technical innovation that was based on a great deception. Bowled by a right-arm bowler it is apparently a leg spinner but it actually turns the other way. Later called a wrong'un or a googly, its first great practitioner was B.J.T. Bosanquet, who perfected it and in his short career won the Ashes for England (1903–04). The English spinner described the secret of his bewitching delivery as 'turning the ball over in the hands by dropping the wrist at the moment of delivery, so that the axis of spin is changed from left to right to right to left, thus converting the spin from an ordinary leg break into an ordinary off break'. In other words, the batsman is deceived into thinking he is getting a ball that is an ordinary leg break, but it turns the other way. In keeping with the natural deceit of the leg spinner Bosanquet, when playing, claimed that the duplicitous ball was a product of accident, the weather or even the state of the pitch. But the 'Bosie', as it became known, was anything but an accident and soon batsmen came to regard it as an unfair delivery.

If the bowler of a googly is exceptional he can hide the delivery from the batsman but the pressure on his shoulder is massive and many a spin bowler has ruined his career attempting to perfect it. Warne's first shoulder injury was said to have been caused when he bowled fifty googlies in a row to wicket-keeper Ian Healy in the practice nets at the Sydney Cricket Ground. There is also another factor to the delivery. The art of bowling a wrong'un can take years to develop. Charlie Grimmett perfected it by bowling it over after over in his backyard, training his indefatigable fox terriers to retrieve the eight balls after he had completed an over and drop them at his feet. The failure to bowl it exactly – there is little room for error – means the batsman can score heavily off it and this in turn can undermine a bowler's confidence to an alarming degree.

For many cricket followers this is the premier ball of a leg spinner and many consider that one is not a true leg spinner unless he can bowl it. But leg spinners have several other types of deliveries in their arsenal, including the top spinner, which does not spin but bounces unnaturally high, and the flipper, of which Warne, before his many injuries, was a master. As Richie Benaud, another great exponent of the delivery, has remarked, 'A flipper puts more strain on your shoulder than any other ball.' The flipper nearly destroyed Richie Benaud's career and approaching his retirement he would turn away from the batsman when collecting his sweater at the end of an over so his grimace of pain as he struggled to put it on couldn't be seen. He describes the flipper as a ball that comes out from underneath the hand: 'If you hold your arm erect with the back of your hand pointing towards the sky and turn your hand anti-clockwise, that would be a leg break, but if you think in terms of the ball being held [by the tips of the first and third fingers] and then "flipped" out upwards and, in effect, clockwise, that is the "flipper". It actually comes from underneath the hand rather than over the top of it.' The batsman thinks he is getting a turning ball but not only does it not turn but it comes on to him abnormally quickly, skidding on to him with little bounce, not unlike a stone being skipped across the water. For some it is called the flipper because it is squeezed or 'flipped' out of the hand and with it comes the sound of the fingers clicking together not unlike clicking your fingers to gain the waiter's attention. It is said that because batsmen knew Warne could bowl this ball he became the master of the double bluff. He would bowl a standard leg spinner but click the fingers of his left hand at the moment of delivery, fooling the batsman into thinking he was about to receive a flipper.

Warne's skill has meant that he has also attacked the batsmen in a method that is uncommon with leg spinners. He has gone around the wicket and directed the ball outside the leg stump, counting on his ability to spin the ball stupendous widths by making it land on the roughage caused by the fast bowlers' foot marks. In some famous cases, as against an extremely good player like Graham Gooch, he has been able to bowl the batsman around his legs. This takes extraordinary accuracy because the ball just has to pitch slightly off length or direction and the batsman can belt it anywhere he likes on the leg side. Warwick Armstrong used the delivery as a defensive tactic in the 1920s, but the cricket laws then allowed a much greater number of fieldsmen on the leg side in those days which meant that many a dreary over went by without a run being scored. Richie Benaud once used it as a desperate tactic against England when it seemed Australia would lose a Test match, but Warne has proved that someone of his talent can use it as an extremely effective offensive method.

Throughout his career Warne has proved he has enormous mental resilience. Resilience in sport is the ability not to give in to yourself. A slow bowler cannot physically threaten a batsman like a fast bowler, but he can psychologically threaten him. But there are times when a batsman flails the bowling and it takes enormous mental resources not to panic. To go through a period where a batsman is thrashing your deliveries to the fence and over it and not mentally crumble is a crucial element in being a leg spinner. Many a leg spinner has been crushed by the punishment a batsman has meted out to him. It takes tremendous willpower to keep coming back ball after ball believing you can defeat the batsman when you can't inflict physical damage on him and all you can do is best him by your skill and unwillingness to give in. Occasionally one can see an exasperated Warne lose his temper and he will bowl a bouncer at the batsman, that, because of its lack of pace, is both comical and innocuous. Leg spin involves the art of patience. The patience is equivalent of the fly-fisherman who dangles and parades a glittering lure patiently waiting for the fish to gobble at what it thinks is merely an innocuous plump fly or tantalisingly close insect, little suspecting that attached to it is a deadly hook. The reason why Warne is a better bowler than was, say, Qadir, is that the Pakistani leg spinner frequently gave way to impatience, the result of which was that he lost control of himself and therefore his bowling.

Through his career Warne has added important

aspects to his craft, so that now he can subtly adjust the speed of his delivery, the ball's trajectory and the bounce. He has also become a master of studying the weakness of his opponent. One cannot comprehend Warne's talent without understanding the point of view of a batsman facing him. And one cannot understand Warne's psychological mastery of many opponents without understanding that cricket, although superficially a team game, is really the individual bowler versus the individual batsman.

In his book *Silence of the Heart – Cricket Suicides*, David Frith points out that cricket has a suicide list far in excess of that of any other sport. The iconography of death is pervasive, from the term for hearing the ball hit the batsman's stumps – the death rattle – to the figure of Father Time with his scythe hovering above the pavilion at Lord's. It is an idiosyncratic sport, especially for the batsman. In golf one hole can be a disaster but the golfer has the next hole at which to do better, baseball has at least three strikes before you're out, a footballer knows he has many chances on the field, a boxer can rise from the canvas to finally win the contest, but a batsman knows that every single ball he faces could be his last, and it's not only that he could be bowled, or caught, run out, given out l.b.w. (leg before wicket), or hit wicket or handled the ball, but the umpire can make grave mistakes, giving him out when he hasn't touched the ball or making an inept l.b.w. decision. The sheer range of how he can get out and the capricious nature of umpiring and the pitch mean that the batsman knows he could be wrongly given out without scoring and that one mistake could cost him his whole career. It is the equivalent of a soccer goalie having to face a penalty kick, not once in a game, but with every single ball he faces. Just the slightest mental doubt can lead to defeat.

Sometimes the opposite can happen and a batsman can enter what some players call 'The Zone'. It's a rare mental state of complete freedom from doubt and self-consciousness. In this state it seems the batsman knows exactly where the ball will bounce and what it will do. It seems that one's body, mind and reflexes are so coordinated that the strokes are played without effort or deliberation. Mark Taylor said that when he scored 334 runs against Pakistan he felt he had entered The Zone and New Zealander Lou Vincent recently scored a century against Australia and could not remember any of his innings, because he had entered a state where he didn't seem to be conscious or aware of how many runs he was scoring or how long he had been batting. Retrospectively he sensed he had the rare sensation that his body and mind were one and the same.

This state or Zone is rare. Mainly batsmen spend much of their time out on the field mentally urging themselves to concentrate, to banish doubt and to focus on nothing else but the next ball. This requires immense concentration, given that an innings can stretch over a day or even two. A batsman is therefore fighting a battle against individual bowlers and himself. It is an extremely solitary mental journey. Poet and novelist P.J. Kavanagh elevates this solitariness to the level of heroism and equates the cricketer's solitary state with that of the poet: 'Like poets, cricketers spend unimaginable numbers of hours doing something near pointless as possible, trying to dig an elusive perfection out of themselves in the face of an infinite number of variables, and as a result a large proportion of their lives belongs to the realm of the mystical. Like poets their faces are deeply engraved by introspection − all crick- eters seem prematurely lined − because they are as deeply locked in a struggle with themselves as they are with the opposition.'

At the back of a batsman's mind all through his career is the numbing thought that the next ball could easily be the last he will ever face. As Frith says: 'It is the uncertainty that excites or more usually erodes. As any serious batsman takes guard, whether he be a Bradman or a colt on trial, he knows that the first ball could get him, bringing with it humiliation. But it is *uncertainty*, day in day out, that plays a sinister beat on the soul.'

And it is this uncertainty that Warne has played on. Facing a fast bowler a batsman has about 0.2 of a second to decide what shot to play, and the stroke will be a mix- ture of skill and reflexes; but facing spin bowling about half that speed the batsman has twice as much time to make up his mind. And that is the problem for many batsmen. Warne actually gives the batsman time to think too much, so he becomes prey to doubts and indecision, which often brings about his downfall. The batsman also knows that Warne will always attack him and never deliberately give him a bad ball to buy his wicket with a catch to distant fielders. He doesn't allow the batsman to mentally drift in his innings by setting easy fields so the batsman can relax, believing there is less chance of getting out. Warne is always coming at you and his fields are set close, so that the surrounding fieldsmen are within touching distance, reminding the batsman that one minor mistake will deliver a catch. It should be said that Warne's bowling average would be better if he weren't so attacking.

As Warne comes up to deliver the ball the batsman has time to look at the spinner's grip, but is the grip part of the deception? Is Warne pretending to bowl a leg spinner when really it will deceive the batsman by turning the opposite way? By the time the ball has left Warne's massive hand the variables increase dramatically. Will the ball drop suddenly or come on? If the ball is thrown higher, for a brief moment, the laws of perception mean that it vanishes from the batsman's eye line and he will have to guess where it will land. Is the ball really going at the speed it seems to be, or is it faster or slower? When it lands will it jump left or right, low or high, or even not spin at all and come low and straight like a pebble skipping across the surface of a lake? Will the ball hit the spike-marks in the pitch left by the fast bowlers' feet? The list goes on and on. Knowing that Warne seems to have endless variations of deliveries and a fabulous talent to deceive causes profound doubt and uncertainty. Many of Warne's victims have lost their wicket through indeterminate strokes based on a fraught sense of not knowing how to react. In other words, he has psychologically overwhelmed the batsman. If any batsman is a perfect example of Warne's mental intimidation it is the South African Daryll Cullinan, a marvellous batsman elsewhere in the world who found himself floundering against the Australian leg spinner. After a time it seemed that even just facing Warne caused Cullinan's brain to seize up. Watching the contest was like seeing a cat toying with a mouse, who at a certain point in the teasing just gives up and waits to be devoured. Cricket may be a team game but for batsmen it is a solitary and even lonely game, and Warne has played on that. In his mind games he has dared his opponents to be mentally tougher than he is but it is the batsmen who have found themselves wanting. Even the exceptions, especially the Indian batsman Tendulkar and a few others, prove the rule. Warne's gift, then, is not only his innate skill but his extraordinary ability to mentally intimidate. That's what makes him so rare. That's what makes him the cricket genius that he is.

3: Just a
Suburban Boy

If there is one seminal image of Australian cricket it is Russell Drysdale's painting *The Cricketers*. It shows two lanky boys playing cricket in an outback town against the side of a building. There is no grass, only a couple of grim gum trees in the background. One of the boys is about to bowl while the batsman raises his bat, in what can only be called a baseballer's pose. A tall, thin man watches the pair from the shade of a veranda. There is something unsettling about the image. The town seems bereft of life and the two boys are devoid of personality, as if they are not human but mysterious symbols, with Drysdale giving the bowler a shadow that deliberately mimics a crucifixion pose. Walter Hutchinson, the English publisher who commissioned the painting, was horrified by it and fired his dealer for incompetence, although later reinstating him when told that Drysdale was an important Australian artist. The painting is now the visual template for the myth of the Australian outback cricketer who is tall, lanky, laconic and naturally athletic. Brought up in the parched outback, his first cricket bat as a child is one sawn out of a hunk of 2 x 4 by his father. With a moth-eaten tennis ball, or one ingeniously carved out of a mallee root, he plays cricket on a dirty makeshift pitch. Firmly attached to this mythical cricketer is the reality of the batting genius Don Bradman, who as a boy practised his cricket skills by hitting a golf ball with a stump against the concrete bottom of a water tank for hour after hour through the scorching Bowral summer days. And as the truth and legend would have it, he emerged from the Australian bush to successfully take on the city's finest bowlers and prove himself the greatest batsman of all time.

But in contemporary cricket it is the exception rather than the rule for a Test cricketer to emerge from the bush, no matter how romantic the notion may still be. Most Test cricketers are suburban boys who have started their cricket in the backyards of quarter-acre suburban blocks. And Warne is no exception, except that his childhood also contained that other iconic Australian landscape – the beach.

Born September 13, 1969 he spent the first five or so years of his life in Ferntree Gully, an outer suburb of Melbourne that twenty or so years before his birth had been untouched by development and still had the romantic lushness of a temperate rainforest. Even now the encroachment of housing development is stymied by a national park and the gorgeous Sherbrooke forest, home to a cornucopia of flora and fauna including the lyrebird. Nothing could be further from the desolate outback of *The Cricketers*, and for Warne's mother, this must have been the closest equivalent to the German countryside she did not remember but had heard her parents talk about after she arrived in Australia in 1949 at the age of three. Brigitte was part of the great post-war boom in immigration that was to transform Australia's economic and then cultural landscape. She spent her childhood on a farm in Apollo Bay, an attractive coastal village along the Great Ocean Road, which winds itself through some of the most dramatic scenery in Australia. She was a natural athlete and aspiring distance runner whose development was retarded by a severe attack of glandular fever at the age of fourteen. In her early twenties she met and married Keith Warne. Both were tall and fit and loved the outdoors and sport. Keith was an especially good tennis player and Brigitte was naturally good at most sports. Shane's love of sport came from the potent genetic brew of both parents and their fostering of his sporting ability and that of his younger brother, Jason.

In the early 'seventies the family shifted to the Melbourne bayside suburbs, first at Hampton and then finally settling at Black Rock, opposite the beach. They are attractive places to bring up children, stubbornly middle class or with the aspiration of being so. The beach is not far away, the house blocks are large, the brick veneer homes spacious, and the gardens luxuriant. This is an area that is really the archetypal Australia. Drive through it today and you will see wide, well-made roads, neat nature strips, two cars in the driveway, and on

the weekends the familiar sight of fathers washing their
cars or mowing the lawns while their sons and daugh-
ters are either at the beach or playing sport on the many
well-kept sports grounds. What is noticeable is how
ethnically white the neighbourhoods are. These suburbs
have pockets of old people's homes, little crime, small
shopping centres rather than malls, and excellent schools
for students whose aspirations are to become doctors,
accountants, businessmen or lawyers. And yet, although
professional ambitions may be high for both the parents
and children, sport is still the crucial social glue. To be
good at a sport is to be admired. Cultural or literary pur-
suits come a distant second to leisure activities. In fact,
the bayside's anti-intellectual attitude is in keeping with
the proud Australian tradition that values sport over
culture, gregarious physical activities over the loner's
absorption in ideas or books. In fact, when Warne
was growing up it would have been difficult to find a
bookshop in the area, or even an ethnic restaurant. The
bayside is white, middle class and charmingly bland. To
use the American word, it is proudly WASP.

Warne's sporting prowess was recognised early. He
played and excelled at tennis, football and cricket and in
the great Australian tradition of brothers like the Chap-
pells, Lees and Waughs, the Warne brothers fought many
an epic cricket battle in their backyard of the quarter-
acre block. These backyard matches and the space and
equipment the boys had symbolised just how affluent
Australia had become. These suburban boys did not go
through the hardships of the pre-World War II era
where boys played makeshift games in narrow inner-city

streets, using a greengrocer's box as stumps, a roughly sawn bat and a ball made of masking tape with fieldsmen warning of approaching cars. Warne's generation was lucky. If he wanted a bat it was bought for him, if he wanted to go to training or play in a football match, his mother or father would drive him there.

As a teenager, Warne's abiding love was not cricket but Australian Rules football. Like most bayside boys he barracked for St Kilda, a team whose oval in Moorabbin always seemed waterlogged and smelly. It was a team that promised much but invariably brought heartache to its supporters. But the team had rare individuals like Trevor Barker. Handsome with long blond locks, Barker had a spectacular leap that catapulted him upwards, like a jack-in-the-box, to pluck a mark above the players below him, briefly hanging in the air, as if defying both gravity and commonsense. In a team of lumpy rhinoceroses he was a gazelle. It's no wonder that Warne idolised him and was desperate to emulate his deeds. The other footballer he admired was Hawthorn's Dermot Brereton, a strong, muscular, flamboyant footballer with an earring, a bushy perm of faux blond hair, a liking for Ferraris, and an aggressiveness that scared many an opponent. Brereton's skills were admirable, but even more admired was his ability to play well in the finals. More than any cricketer – even though he admired Dennis Lillee – these two footballers were to profoundly influence Warne. There was not only their talent and charisma but their appearance. One of the most pleasing moments of Warne's budding football career was when Barker gave him the nickname

'Hollywood' when he joined the St Kilda football club.

If you don't understand Warne's enthusiasm for Australian Rules football then you will never quite appreciate his special ability. Australian Rules is the only football game that doesn't have an off-side rule (that is when one is illegally between the ball and the opposing team's goal line). Basically invented by Tom Wills in the middle of the nineteenth century to keep cricketers fit during winter, it is a free-wheeling, constantly attacking, high-scoring game with a very Australian disdain for the defensive. Its trademark is the spectacular high mark, which has also given it the derogatory nicknames of 'aerial ping-pong' and 'aerial ballet' and it is dismissed by rugby enthusiasts, whose game resembles not so much football as homoerotic wrestling on the run.

Both of Warne's heroes were forwards and as such he was to model his combative attitude on their attacking play. When he later captained the Australian one-day team for a short but successful period it was easy to see that his competitive aggression, geeing-up of his fellow players, and infectious enthusiasm owed everything to Australian Rules football. Of course, to say that is to say he is merely Victorian. As many a Sydneysider has discovered to his amazement, a winter conversation in Melbourne that does not include the topic of football as one of its major ingredients is rare and regarded as almost an act of sacrilege. Even women, who make up a large proportion of the game's spectators, always have at least a token football club to barrack for, even if it is of no interest to them. The game is closer to pagan religion than sport and Warne's burning ambition to play it at the highest level was a familiar dream to many a Victorian schoolboy.

Like many sports-mad youths Warne was a reluctant student and in his autobiography he says that he regarded school as 'a pain in the neck'. He took no interest in study or literature, the latter of which so totally bored him that he says that he never read a book all the way through. He first went to school at Sandringham Primary, where the three constants of his life were already in evidence: a devotion to sport, a love of being the centre of attention, and a sense of the mischievous, to the extent of, as one friend remarked, 'taking the piss out of teachers'.

In 1982 he went to Hampton High, a double-storey school with large gardens, surrounded by Californian bungalows and, in a very Australian touch, with streets named after famous World War I battles. Determined to stand out he dyed his hair blond, and fashion dictated its change from shaggy to spiky to the mullet. Later he added an earring, which upset his parents: 'My parents freaked. My mother said I looked like a girl and Dad reckoned I looked like a poofter.' Given he is very sensitive about being called a poofter, even now, you can gauge the importance of the fashionable statement of an earring. It's hard to picture now, but in his middle teenage years he was a lithe figure with two long legs that resembled stilts. In his late teenage years he filled out into something approaching the solid form of recent years. His blond hair, earring, sporting prowess and happy-go-lucky, even larrikin, ways were greatly appealing not only to the boys of his circle. Girls were very attracted to him, and Warne was considered to be a bit of a ladies' man.

After three years as an average to poor student at Hampton High he won a sports scholarship to Mentone Grammar, which was close to the beach and had spacious gardens and sporting facilities and was surrounded by churches and many lovely examples of Edwardian houses. Warne is one of the few recent Test cricketers to attend a private school. Except for a brief interest in bookkeeping and accountancy ('I lost complete interest in it when we started to learn contract law') and his continuing lack of interest in English, he managed to scrape through his years at Mentone.

Like many of his mates he was drawn to the beach culture of the bayside suburbs. He showed no interest in the posh and strenuous activity of sailing, which is a feature of the area. His interests were simple and uncomplicated: swimming, sunbaking, smoking cigarettes on the sly, ogling girls in flimsy bikinis and, of course, the necessary social lubricant of alcohol. Nothing much has changed. You can still see these teenage boys hanging out around the shopping centres on a summer night, teasing one another on the beach, surreptitiously smoking dope, sneaking into one of the many large hotels in the area. These are suburbs where boys and girls start going out together in their late teens and end up marrying and staying in the area. It is as if their lives are determined by the craggy cliff tops, the long winding paths leading down to the flat white beaches where everything is bland and democratic. No-one dresses up, boys wear the daggy beach uniform of board shorts and the girls the flimsy wrap-around for the walk back to their close-by homes and the shower to wash off the sand, protective zinc and suntan oil. Nothing is too arduous and days drift by in a haze of indolence, or if the teenagers know the words, a daily sybaritic supplication to the sun, sea and sand. This is middle-class, middlebrow Australia. This is a world that seems cut off from stress, ideology, multicultural tensions and the excitement of difference. Travelling through it there is a sense that the rest of the world, with all its problems and poverty and spiritual concerns, does not exist. It is a cocoon of middle-class privilege and limited concerns. It is a world of almost suffocating dullness and as such has been shunned by Australian poets and novelists except to satirise it. It's probably too easy to criticise it or mock it. But for most Australians these bayside suburbs are an idyll and they unmistakably created Warne's social limits and flat cultural horizons. The bayside sculptured and shaped him and nothing else has been able to take its place. The boy who wandered its streets and swam in the sea and understood that within the confines of a sports oval he could find happiness is the man you get today.

The bayside beach culture held a greater attraction for him than that of cricket. Football and the beach were his priorities. An enervating day playing cricket in the hot sun and chasing cricket balls in the heat had limited appeal for him. But he did play. Regarding his interest in leg spin, Warne says there was no single defining moment when he, to quote him, 'saw the light'. If anything he viewed himself as a batsman who liked to slog the ball as hard as possible and who occasionally bowled. He was thought by some to lack potential as a leg spinner and some who saw him bowl during these years told him to give it up. He was taught the rudimentary leg spin grip by Ron Cantlon, a coach at East Sandringham, and there were others from whom he gleaned more, and this is a feature of Warne's career: he is a patient and good listener to anyone who is prepared to impart their cricket knowledge. However, for all he has learnt, he basically believes he had an innate, natural ability. In his middle teenage years he was content to play for Mentone Grammar and then the Brighton Cricket Club at sub-district level. Yet even in these early days the traits of determination and inner confidence were apparent. A Brighton cricketer, Raj Krishnan, said of him: 'He never seemed to feel pressure … some people do and tend to go back in their shell, but Shane got more aggressive.'

But cricket was merely a diversion that he made certain wouldn't impinge on his deeply felt dream of playing league football. He played two seasons for St Kilda, playing well for the Under-19s. Near the end of the first season he faced a dilemma. He had come down with a virus but was asked to play for the reserves, the penultimate step to playing in the seniors. Of course he said he could play and hoped he would impress the selectors, but the flu was worse than he expected and he performed badly. Warne is still convinced that this listless performance told against him when the club made the decision to drop him from the playing list for 1989, but in reality the problem was more basic. He was too short for the post he coveted, full forward, and too slow to play in other parts of the forward line. And, most importantly, the coach Gary Colling deemed he was overweight and lazy. This was the most disappointing time of his life. He was crushed. He could have played for the VFA, the league just below the VFL/AFL in standard, but he had too much pride. His dream of playing for St Kilda, something brightly polished by hope and potential, was now gone and there was nothing in its place. Besides the devastating blow there was something else that Warne would miss and that was the camaraderie of football. Always a gregarious man who finds great satisfaction in being part of a team, he felt the loss of football's mateship, tribal behaviour and shared goals to be shattering.

Not only was his football career over but his personal life was going nowhere. Because he had no academic qualifications, he found himself drifting alarmingly from job to job, depending upon the kindness of family friends for employment. The results were slapstick (backing a truck into a wall, unable to put a waterbed together), boredom (he gave up learning the jewellery business because it was 'too precise and laborious') or farcical (delivering pizzas which was the equivalent of letting a glutton loose at a free smorgasbord).

He was still playing cricket, now for St Kilda Second XI, but like his aimless employment record it seemed to offer no future. It was a cricket friend, Rick Gough, who was to help Warne out of his stagnant situation. He suggested that both of them go to England to play cricket. After many letters of rejection they were accepted by the minor league Imperial Club in Bristol. Warne bowled and batted particularly well during the season and his uncomplicated charm attracted the locals.

The touchstones of his memory of his time playing with the Imperial Club, instead of cricket grounds, are a roll call of pubs such as Busby's, the George (which he was fond of because the owners treated him like a son and were 'like my parents away from home'), Town's Talk and other pubs which became a blur given that 'Thursday to Sunday were just drinkathons'. In fact he says that he and Gough became 'drinking machines'. This is, of course, in the proud tradition of such players as Rod Marsh and David Boon who have had to be helped off planes at Heathrow after breaking drinking records for the flight from Australia to England. It was not only the pint jugs of beer that played havoc with his weight but the English fatty foods. He returned to Australia so plump that his wiry, fit father did not recognise him at the airport. To make matters worse, he found that he had been relegated from the St Kilda Second XI to the Thirds.

His demotion shocked him into the realisation of just where he stood in life. He had no job prospects, no future in football and as far as cricket was concerned he seemed to be going backwards. All he had was one great ability – he could spin a cricket ball. His grasp of the craft may have been primitive, but he knew that his last opportunity to succeed in life lay in something as simple as a small round object that is made out of a cube of cork around which twine is wound to produce a sphere, which in turn is covered by two hemispheres of red leather and which are stitched together to create a hard ball with a raised seam. For the first time he took some responsibility for himself. He started to train as he hadn't in England, but his weight was slow to come off. He hoped the extra effort he was putting in would help him rise up through the ranks, but he seemed doomed to languish in the lowly Thirds. It must have occurred to him many times that he should give up trying and join his mates playing social cricket, but underneath that flabby exterior and the bottle-blond locks that did not so much bedazzle his team-mates as amuse them was a young man determined to do better in life than he had so far. He practised as he had never done before, trying to control his prodigious turn while improving his accuracy. Even though he was not taking many wickets he was promoted to the Firsts when the resident leg spinner injured his hand. He played a couple of games and again did not take many wickets. Yet he did impress some of his team-mates and opposition players. There was something immensely exciting about his potential. It was not only his ability to turn the ball and land it accurately, but for knowledgeable cricketers there is something exhilarating about hearing a ball from a spin-ner fizzing through the air like an angry wasp as the raised seam of the ball brutally attacked the air currents; it indicates that the ball has been given a tremendous 'tweak' from the wrist and with it comes the vicious and sudden lateral jump off the pitch. But he wasn't really fulfilling his potential and there were many more suc-cessful bowlers than he in the district competition. However, what he didn't know at the time was that

Australian cricket officials were engaged in an increasingly desperate search to find a leg spinner who could win Tests for Australia.

For over a decade the West Indians, under both Clive Lloyd and Viv Richards, proved themselves the supreme Test cricket teams. They inflicted heavy defeats on Australia, the major reason being their brutal four-man pace attack. Yet occasional West Indian defeats by Australia had a common denominator – it was a spinner who won the match, whether it was Bob Holland in 1984–85 or Allan Border in 1988–89 when he amazed both himself and the West Indians by taking eleven wickets to help win the Test match in Sydney. Other nations don't quite have the same attitude to leg spinners as Australia. English, South African and West Indian teams are attracted to spin as a defensive tactic. That's why they prefer off-spinners. It's a skill that is more easily learnt than leg spin. The grip enables one to control the delivery better and even though the ball doesn't spin as much and, turning into the right-handed batsmen instead of away, is not as dangerous a delivery, the off spinner is thought to be less expensive and in tight situations he can keep down the flow of runs. But from a young age Australian boys are taught to despise off spinners. There is something defensive about the skill. It reeks of English tactics and a sort of sporting cowardice. Australian selectors have the same attitude and are always on the lookout for a leg spinner. So despite his average figures, Warne was fast-tracked and sent to the newly opened Cricket Academy at the Australian Institute of Sport in Adelaide.

Warne's eight months there were to be controversial. As far as he is concerned he may have been in his early twenties but the Academy treated him like a schoolboy. He chaffed against what he saw as the regimentation of the place which involved being disciplined for what he thought were minor infractions. Having to get up at seven in the morning was bad enough, but being forced to undergo a strenuous day-long training program plus being told what time to go to bed was anathema to him. He stayed out at night, drank and partied. He was a 'fun guy', whose eating habits horrified his physically fit team-mates, but he so endeared himself to them that they voted him the most popular player. He tested the patience of the authorities as much as he could. He learnt to develop flight and control from one of the few coaches he liked, Terry Jenner, who was recently out of gaol after serving time for embezzlement. It is a common thread through Warne's life that if you can impart something useful to him, you earn his respect.

Most people at the Academy realised he had a special talent, but how to harness it, given that, as he has stated, all he wanted to do was spin the ball as far as possible and have a good time? Sometimes he was thoughtless and pushed too far. There was a notorious incident on a team trip to Darwin where, being the team lair as usual around the hotel pool, he made what he thought were funny sexual remarks and gestures to three female Asian university students. Appalled by Warne's crudity, the students complained and an official from the Academy had to fly up to Darwin to forestall a police investigation into the incident. In his autobiography

Warne refers to it as 'a pool prank', but it was seen as more than that by those in charge of the Academy who were not the first people to assume that Warne may have talent but that his boofhead behaviour subverted it. The prank so rankled with them that he was forbidden to go on an Academy tour to Sri Lanka in 1990.

Warne is someone who finds it incredibly difficult to put himself in the position of another person. Because he doesn't act from spite he is incapable of seeing that his behaviour hurts or disturbs others. It is their problem, not his. He can admit, as he did, that in rebelling against what he thought was 'total discipline' he was 'a bit of an idiot', but as far as he is concerned if there is no deliberate malice involved, why should the victims of his pranks take it so personally? With an attitude like that it's easy to understand his befuddlement and then anger at being left out of the Sri Lankan tour. The situation between the Academy officials and Warne festered. He realised that it was just a matter of time before he was expelled. He was smart enough to know he had better resign, which he did.

Back in his home State he was thrust into the Victorian Second XI, again as a way of fast-tracking his career as a leg spinner. He played several games and again fortune favoured him. Two State players were chosen for a Test tour to the West Indies and a place became vacant for him in the Victorian team. Looking at his poor statistics to that point in his career it is easy to be puzzled at why he made it into the Victorian team. He played a match and, again, his figures were unimpressive and he was dropped. He was chosen to join the Australia

B team to tour Zimbabwe, where for the first time he showed his potential by taking seven wickets in an innings against the Zimbabwe national team. Some still felt, though, that his potential was being sabotaged by his impatience. By this stage Australian officials, who were giving him all the help they could to try to develop him into a match-winning bowler, must have been exasperated. Other players not so favoured by the Australian desire to have a champion leg spinner must have been envious. What is extraordinary is that in returning to Australia after a mediocre tour he made it quite clear to the Victorian selectors that if they did not choose him he would scamper across the border into NSW. The sheer hide of Warne's non-too-subtle blackmail is an indication that he was now well aware he was being favoured by the national selectors. His confidence in his own ability, though not justified by much he had done on the field, was typical of his chutzpah. But at the same time he was continuing to ask and learn from anyone who could help him. One of the most important things he discovered was to bowl slower. He found that when he did he turned the ball much more. His approach to the wicket was no longer a run-up but what looked like an amble or stroll that finished with a couple of quick steps that contained little momentum, so that when he bowled the ball, he put such an effort into it, that it was as if his arm were being wrenched out of its shoulder socket.

Luck continued to flow his way. The Prime Minister, Bob Hawke, quite a talented cricketer himself in his youth, chose Warne to play for the Prime Minister's XI in a one-day match against the West Indies. His figures were again average. Then he was chosen for an Australian XI against the West Indies down in Hobart. For all his confidence and bravado with the Victorian selectors, Warne must have realised that his chances of becoming a Test cricketer were looking decidedly shaky and this was probably one of the last chances he had of showing people he was capable of playing cricket at an élite level. If he bowled badly in this match it was likely he would be forgotten and the Australian officials would chase after some other young leg spinner. But Warne bowled well. Most of his wickets were against batting duffers, but they were still the best figures he had had for a while. What pleased the selectors was that he had bowled well against the West Indians. The problem was that they would not be touring again until the following season and the earliest Test match they could blood him in was the Third Test against India, currently touring Australia.

Warne spent the Second Test between Australia and India gobbling junk food and drinking beer with his mates in the Members' Stand of the Melbourne Cricket Ground. He had vague hopes he might be picked for the Test team but no great expectations. During the game, fat, cheerful Warne, carrying a meat pie and a couple of beers, and looking very much like a typical suburban yobbo, bumped into Bob Simpson, former Test player, present coach and fitness nut who was horrified to see what Warne was eating and how porky he was. Ian McDonald, the media manager, equally stunned, said ruefully, 'Just take it easy, son.' All Warne could do was giggle good-naturedly and head off back to his mates. A few hours later McDonald rang him at home and told him he was chosen to play in the Third Test. Warne's rise had been phenomenal and, for the huge majority of cricketer followers who had never heard of him as he prepared to play his first Test, almost inexplicable.

4: The Only Way is Up

To be selected for the Australian cricket team is of enormous importance to anyone who has been chosen. Prime Minister John Howard spoke for many people when he once said that the job of being Australian cricket captain is more important than that of being Prime Minister. Just to receive the Australian cricket cap signifying you have been selected to play for Australia is a great honour. The baggy green cap is revered by all players. On first receiving his cap, Test batsman Paul Sheahan wore it to bed. Justin Langer says: 'It sends shivers down the back of the spine when your team-mate is presented with the baggy green for the first time.' And for Warne it was no different. He has always referred to it as the proudest moment of his life. The party to celebrate his selection was held at his parents' house and he drank so much and was so hungover the next day he had to stall the media so he could vomit in the toilet. On the television news he looked seedy but cheerful, with a golden spiky haircut that resembled an echidna sleeping on his head. Then he flew to Sydney to join the team, most of whom he didn't know. It seemed to him that it was not so much a step up but merely a widening of the circle of drinking mates, because on New Year's night two of Australia's best cricketers, Boon and Marsh, took him to a hotel in The Rocks and he spent the night drinking with them. 'I thought "Gee, this is all right". I don't know how many stubbies we ended up having. I've got no idea but it was a hell of a lot. I just thought "This Test cricket is all right".'

At least he had a day to recover before the Test started on January 3. For most of the spectators and huge majority of television viewers the sight of the unknown Warne coming on to bowl was alarming. This was no svelte spinner like the handsome, lean Richie Benaud, with shirt buttons open to reveal a tanned, muscular chest; instead they saw the 97-kilogram Warne, whose several chins and spare tyres made him from a distance resemble a Michelin Man wrapped in white sheets. As he came on to bowl his first ball in Test cricket his team-mates' teasing (the casual act of cruelty we Australians are so good at) was ringing in his ears. One tintinnabulation, of ominous forewarning, were his captain's 'Hey, Warnie, don't do a Johnny Watkins on us,' a reference to the most inauspicious début a leg spinner has ever made in Test cricket, when in 1977 the anxious Watkins found he could barely land the ball on the pitch, let alone direct it at the stumps.

The pitch itself was slow and the ball did not bounce. Because of an injury to the tall, thin Bruce Reid, the fast bowler who seemed more a cartilagenous outline than a man of flesh and bone and was prone to physical breakdowns that finally ruined his career, Warne was forced to bowl earlier and longer than he would have reasonably expected. And he was bowling against the Indians who are the best players of leg spin in the world.

It was not so much Warne's bulbous bulk that intrigued spectators but his run-up, which seemed to be nothing more than a waddle up to the wicket, and as he came into bowl his tongue stuck out of his mouth like a schoolboy confronting the mysteries of an algebraic formula for the first time. The wrench of his arm and simultaneous grunt of effort were merely an amusing coda to the whole of his bowling approach. He was so nervous and perspired so profusely that he could barely grip the ball during the first over. Content to just get the ball on a length and directed at the stumps, he started reasonably well, but as Indian opener Sanjay Manjrekar, who faced Warne's first ball in Test cricket, has stated, in no way did he or the rest of the Indian team consider they were watching a champion in the making. 'Normally a great player will show you signs early that there is something special about them. I never got that feeling with Shane.' Manjrekar is not exaggerating, because it was obvious during the match that Warne held no special dangers for the Indian batsmen. They gave his bowling a terrible hiding, especially Sachin Tendulkar who made a century, and Ravi Shastri, who scored a double century and in the process hit Warne with such carefree abandon that one hoped that Border, Warne's captain, would take him out of the attack. He couldn't as he was down one strike bowler. It was uncomfortable to watch Warne bowl. He tried to hide his frustration behind a blank genial expression, but you could see in his eyes the pain of undergoing such public humiliation. It was not only the crowd at the ground who watched silently as he struggled to unsettle the Indian batsmen, let alone grab a wicket, but the television viewers. He knew that everyone at the ground or in a pub watching the game would be mentally saying the same thing: *The fat boy can't cut it at the élite level.*

But there was no reason for him to bother about what the spectators were thinking because he was obviously harsher on himself and was thinking the same thing. He didn't so much bowl the ball as willed it in the direction he wanted it to go. After a time you knew he thought he wasn't going to get a wicket. All he wanted was for the Indians to stop plundering his bowling. After each four or six his eyes dulled. He licked his lips, which were dry with effort and tension. Every over was begun with grim determination but by the time it was finished his eyes looked haunted and indeed he *was* haunted, haunted by failure. There seemed to be nothing he could do that would earn him a wicket. The Indian batsmen made it clear they didn't respect his skill. All he wanted was to hide, but his captain kept throwing him the ball. Never had Warne felt more naked and more exposed as a fraud or wannabe. The sheer confidence and gall he had shown up to now evaporated in the enervating day. By the end of it he was a hollow man, as if determination, inspiration and self-belief had been scooped out of him. The giveaway of inner turmoil in sportsmen is always the eyes. The body may be going through the motions, as was Warne's, but the eyes were blank and uninvolved, as if they were covered with a film of defeat so profound that opponents and spectators no longer existed as people but only intimidating phantoms. The ball that was once so easy to deliver and spin that it seemed an extension of the hand was now merely a round lump that once released seemed to obey its own obtuse logic, which in no way reflected the grip that once held it. In Test cricket there is such a thing as territorial privilege, that is, within the boundary ropes you must justify your entitlement to be playing there at that particular élite level, and if you can't justify your presence then you are mocked, not necessarily with words but with deeds. It takes great self-belief to be publicly thrashed and yet be able to say to yourself that you belong at this level and are the equal or better of everyone else on the field. On that day Warne felt he wasn't entitled to be on the Sydney ground and every scoring shot off his bowling mocked him.

He even dropped a catch off his own bowling, but finally he took a wicket when Shastri, having grown tired, holed out to be caught near the fence. Warne was delighted to have taken his first wicket in Test cricket but his figures were dreadful – one wicket for one hundred and fifty runs. If that were not enough he had to join his captain near the end of the fifth day and bat out the remaining overs to stop Australia losing the match. The pressure was intense and Border, seeing the glazed look of fear in the 22-year-old's eyes, said in his usual inimitable gruff fashion: 'Come on, dig in and fucking don't get out, you're playing for Australia.' And Warne didn't, managing to stay not out for the next fifteen minutes. At the end of the match a disheartened Warne resigned himself to the fact that he had at least played in one Test match, which was more than most could say.

The old leg spinner Bill O'Reilly wrote that he was prepared to accept Warne 'with open arms to the important spin society', but his comments seemed more wish fulfilment than any realistic hope the youngster would succeed. Others were less hopeful or forgiving, with several reporters calling his début as 'a shocker'. I remember leaving the ground thinking that it would be the first and last time I would see Warne play Test cricket. Despite his cheerful and optimistic banter to friends and the press, Warne knew deep down that it was indeed a disastrous début, and he was to admit later that not only did he feel he wasn't ready or good enough to play Test cricket but that maybe he didn't have the skill to play at that level.

The selectors must have thought he could play at Test level because they chose him for the Fourth Test against India in Adelaide. Australia won by 38 runs in a tight contest but Warne failed to claim a wicket in either innings. In fact, in the final run chase, Warne bowled so poorly that he was helping India towards a certain victory and had to be taken off. For Bob Simpson, the Australian coach, it was quite obvious: 'Shane knew little about taking wickets, relied on his natural talent and bowled without expectation. His body language was poor and he seemed to feel he'd done the job when the ball left his hand.'

It was no surprise when Warne was dropped from the team for the final Test but things grew worse, he was even dropped from the Victorian team. His sense of frustration was growing: 'Basically I wanted to be a footy player. It wasn't until I was thirteen or fourteen that I started playing junior cricket and was shown the basics of leg spin. I've no idea why I stuck with it. I could never land the bloody thing then.' Just why he was sticking with it when he had been such a conspicuous failure is probably related to several things. He was tantalisingly close to playing a sport at an élite level, he felt he had let people down, including those like the selectors who had faith in him and he knew that his ability had the potential to offer him personal salvation. So now he made a conscious decision to seek out former players and absorb all the advice he could. His patent determination to improve impressed the selectors, and much to the amazement of many a cricketer follower, Warne, with the Test career figures of one wicket for 228 runs, and soon after being dropped to 12th man in the State team, was chosen for the tour to Sri Lanka.

Despite his hard work in the nets and humble attempts to improve his craft there was still something lax about Warne, as if he thought it was his right to play for Australia. His mentor Terry Jenner vividly sensed this. If there was one person Warne respected it was Jenner, a former leg spin bowler, who, despite being talented played only nine Tests for Australia. The only one of Jenner's Tests people remember is for the wrong reasons when in the 1970–71 series against England he was struck on the head by a short ball from John Snow. The event provoked an ugly crowd scene, prompting a yob in a towelling hat to lean across the boundary fence and grab the fast bowler by the shirt, which in turn provoked the English captain Ray Illingworth to lead his side from the ground. Warne met Jenner when the former Test cricketer was on parole. Jenner had tried to keep a gambling problem hidden, but the addiction is a treadmill of infrequent wins and frequent losses that is in itself a treadmill to oblivion. In order to pay his gambling debts he stole and was sentenced to six and a half years for embezzling more than $10,000. Part of his personal rehabilitation started when he was asked to work at the Cricket Academy with the spinners. He had been told about Warne and warned that 'he's a bit hard to handle'. His first memory of him is of 'a chubby, cheeky bloke with blond spiked hair'. As far as he was concerned Warne may have been rebellious but he was not 'sinister'. The two got on well, although Jenner was sometimes amazed at Warne's lack of knowledge about the history of the game: 'I'd say to him on occasions, "Shane, Test cricket didn't start in 1991. You did." ' Warne respected Jenner and soaked up his advice, especially that of the mental game a spinner has to win.

As far as Warne was concerned, Jenner's involvement with himself and other young cricketers was a vital part of his rehabilitation. But Jenner saw similarities between himself and his protégé, a sort of cheeky larrikin impulse, a 'touch of the maverick' and an attitude that had no sense of the future or of the consequences of his actions. Jenner had been a cricketer of great promise, like Warne, but hadn't lived up to his potential. He saw in Warne the same thoughtlessness that had led him to prison and he was in the perfect position to warn his pupil of the pitfalls. What Jenner knew, perhaps better than anyone else, was that because Warne was such a natural, everything had come too easily to him. The selectors had shown uncommon faith, his entry into Test cricket had been absurdly effortless and now, even though his efforts in his first two Tests were sub-standard, he had been chosen to go to Sri Lanka and he seemed to accept it as his God-given right. Jenner realised that Warne had to lose weight and by becoming leaner would show his many detractors that he was serious about his cricket. One night when Warne arrived with an armful of booze an angry Jenner launched into a speech he had brooded on for a while, telling him he was drinking and partying too much and was over-weight. '[I told] him how he hadn't made the necessary sacrifices to be playing for Australia. I didn't want him to make the mistakes that I did. There wasn't a decent wrist spinner under thirty-five good enough to be play-ing. I wanted him to go home, put his head down and really see how good his best was. He knew that I under-stood exactly what he was going through. We were so alike in many ways.' Needing to be liked was high on the list. The talk unsettled Warne. Not only was his mentor angry with him – and Jenner is right, Warne hates to be disliked – but he had lectured him and if there is anything Warne loathes it is to be lectured to. Soaking up cricket information is well and good, but to be lectured to, well, that is too much like school or the conformist Cricket Academy for his liking. Stubbornly, Warne wasn't going to allow Jenner the high moral ground and merely told his mentor that 'Well, I can't promise I'm going home and do something about it.'

It was left at that. Jenner heard nothing from Warne until two weeks later, when Warne's mother rang: 'I don't know what you said, Terry, but it's working. He's running every morning bar Tuesday when he goes to golf.' Warne had embarked on a strenuous daily exercise regime, even to the extent of giving up beer, that was to see his weight drop off, until he reached his football playing weight of 82 kilos. The transformation was startling. His amorphous plump face was sculpted into something handsome, his body had a muscular tone to it and he was faster and more mobile. Now that Warne had the physique he wanted, a body which would not wilt in the steamy enervating conditions of Sri Lanka, he had no excuses if he did not succeed there.

Sri Lanka was not a popular destination. There was the interminable civil war with Tamil extremists and such was the mindless violence conducted by the terrorists that the New Zealand Test team abandoned a tour in 1987 after a bomb went off in Colombo, killing over a hundred people, and a planned Australian tour was aborted in 1989 when Foreign Affairs decided it was too dangerous. The 1992 tour was considered to be less risky. It was important, because cricket authorities were concerned that tours of the subcontinent were too infrequent, and Test cricket was beginning to lose its significance because of the growing success of the one-day game. For Australia, Sri Lanka was a determined first step in trying to overcome the bogey of touring the region. For decades, especially in Pakistan, Australian teams had folded under the pressure of perceived bad umpiring, poor food and unforgiving climate. Even though Australia had beaten England in the previous Ashes tour, its record against the West Indies and in the subcontinent was poor. Allan Border had been a reluctant captain but was trying to develop the team into something special. Ordinarily, a three-match Test series against a minnow team like Sri Lanka would have resulted in an easy series victory, but Border himself was out of form, and it was rumoured that his captaincy was on the line. He had a reasonable off spinner in Greg Matthews, whose bowling seldom won a Test match, and whose new spinning partner was Shane Warne, who was considered lucky to be in the team.

Watching Warne in the first innings of the First Test in Colombo, even his supporters in the team must have doubted him. Podgy, short Ranatunga took to Warne, hitting him for 29 runs in just three overs. And after six overs he was giving away seven runs per over. After his spell he had no wickets at a cost of 107 runs. He was replaced and had to watch helplessly as the other Australian bowlers tried to contain the rampant Sri Lanka batsmen. As demoralised Warne was to say to Border before Australia batted for a second time: 'I really sweated to get right for this. I didn't have a drink for four months. And for what?' All Border could offer was his belief that he had worked hard and it would pay off. Greg Matthews told Warne that if the selectors did not think he could do the job, they wouldn't have chosen him. Both pieces of advice may sound like sportsmen's clichés but the fact that both men still believed in him mattered greatly. In a team game like cricket or football a player is generally doing two things simultaneously. He is trying to do his best and trying not to let the side down. It's a double burden, especially when you know, or think you know, that there are team members who are questioning your worth in the team, just as you are.

Set 181 runs to win, Sri Lanka started off well and as the day wore on more and more spectators arrived at the ground to witness their country's rare win against Australia. By the time Sri Lanka was 23 runs from victory they had three wickets in hand and if the team batted sensibly, they would win. It was then that Border made a courageous decision. Matthews was bowling well at one end, containing the batsmen, but the Australians needed to take the three remaining wickets. He decided to let Warne bowl. It stunned everyone, including the bowler himself. After all, he had only one Test wicket for over 300 runs, had been belted around the field in the first innings and had no confidence to speak of. So much so, that when he walked in to bowl his first ball, he was more nervous than on his début. Not only was his position in the team at stake, but Border's captaincy would be severely questioned if Warne failed. And then there was the question of winning the game. One bad over and Sri Lanka would be so close to winning that it would be a formality. The superb batsman, Gurusinha, was fortunately at the other end when

Warne bowled to Wickramesinghe. The first two balls were accurate and the batsman didn't look comfortable. The garrulous, chirpy Matthews was loudly encouraging Warne, shouting, 'C'mon, Suicide' (the nickname Matthews gave him from the INXS song 'Suicide Blonde'). The third ball Warne bowled, the Sri Lankan hit a catch to Mark Waugh at cover. Warne was excited and relieved but irked when his fellow Victorian player, Dean Jones, rushed up not to congratulate but to mock him with 'Well done, mate, your average is 230 now'. In the following over the new batsman Anurasiri mishit a drive and that supreme fieldsman Mark Waugh again held the close-in catch. And again Jones (whose favourite topic of conversation, according to team-mates, is either himself or cricket, but preferably both blurred into the one topic) hurried up to Warne to chortle: 'Mate, your average's come down to 150 now.' Retrospectively, Warne sees that Jones may have been trying to relax the spinner by being funny, but at the time the comments rankled badly. Warne hates to be laughed at.

There was one more wicket to get. The crowd, which had been vocal and loud, was now silent and tense, sensing disappointment. From the other end Gurusinha realised that Warne was bowling exception-ally well, 'turning the ball at almost right angles'. The last batsman, Madurasinghe, survived the over and eight runs were scored off Matthews' next over. But Gurusinha couldn't get down to the other end to face the increasingly dangerous Warne. The first ball of Warne's next over Madurasinghe hit a soft catch to

Matthews. It was over and Australia had won by sixteen runs. His figures were marvellous. He had bowled thirteen balls for no runs and taken three wickets that won the game for Australia. Back home in Australia few people knew about the Test, as it wasn't on television and the newspapers didn't consider the series of importance. But it soon filtered back that Shane Warne had finally done something to justify his place in the team.

Naturally, Warne was delighted by what he had accomplished, but he knew it was Border's bravery in choosing him to bowl at the end that was the significant factor in his redemption as a Test cricketer: '[He] had clearly seen something in my character which I didn't realise was there myself. He said afterwards that I held my hand up when it mattered. In reality the captain yanked it out of my pocket.' Greg Matthews was more evocative: '[Warne] could have just crawled into a corner and died. But he won us a Test match. And he didn't do it darting them in. He won it giving them a rip and tossing them up.' In other words, Warne had dared the batsmen to hit him and hit him hard. He could have easily bowled fast and defensively. It was one of the first signs that, despite his lack of confidence, he had not lost that competitive, aggressive streak that people recognised in him from his childhood. He was also astute enough to realise that he hadn't won the Test match — Matthews had done more to deserve that accolade. Still there was a profound relief that he could justify his place in the team: 'At least I didn't feel like excess luggage.'

He returned to Australia knowing that he had a long way to go and that news of his prowess in a far-off land would mean little to Australians. He was proved right. The national selectors still had reservations about his temperament, and accordingly left him out of the First Test against the West Indies in Brisbane, believing that because the boundaries were the shortest in Australia the West Indian batsmen would score heavily against him and therefore ruin his confidence. To those who hadn't witnessed his coolness under pressure in Sri Lanka, it probably seemed a reasonable precaution. The trouble was, as cantankerous Border was to complain after not being able to force a victory against the West Indians in Brisbane, that if Warne had been playing, Australia would have won. For most Australians this seemed fanciful, especially if you glanced at his bowling figures and saw that the leg spinner had taken only four wickets in four Tests at almost 100 runs each.

Warne was chosen for the Boxing Day Test in his home town of Melbourne. To perform well was vital. The national selectors had persevered with him even though there seemed no logic in their reasoning, just blind allegiance to a bowler who might be able to successfully challenge the West Indian batsmen. Like a lot of Australian cricket followers, the West Indian team had scant respect for Warne and thought what slender reputation he had was exaggerated. Warne himself knew that so far his best bowling figures in Test cricket had been against tail enders. Now he would have to prove himself against some of the best batsmen in the world, including the captain Richie Richardson. Richardson's graceful, effortless batting was clearly distinguishable from his former captain, Viv Richards' brutal aggression, but what he learnt from him was the cultivation of sulky condescension towards any opponent whom he considered inferior.

The partisan Victorian spectators gave local boy Warne a wonderful reception when he walked out to bat. He scored only one, but worse was to come; the only wicket he could take was when he bowled the tail ender Ambrose, whose skill with the bat was the equivalent of giving Homer Simpson the run of a nuclear reactor. When the West Indians went out to bat a second time they needed 359 to win. Warne, whose Test figures were now a feeble five wickets in five Tests at 88 runs each, was thoroughly depressed. Rarely obviously dispirited in front of fellow players (like many Australian blokes he keeps his tantrums and depressions for the privacy of his own home), he was almost catatonic with anxiety before going onto the field. Here, in his home town, he feared he was going to play his last Test, thoroughly humiliated by the West Indian batsmen. He would be walking out to play a team which Australia hadn't won a series against since 1976, and his thrashing would be totally public, in front of 15,000 people at the ground, some of them family and friends, and millions watching on television. Ian Healy, the wicket-keeper, could read the signs of panic and dread in the young spinner's face and asked him what he was thinking. Warne confessed he was frightened, not only about being hit all over the ground, as the Indians had done to him in his début Test, but about it happening in front of his friends and him never playing for Australia again. Healy, who kept a diary throughout his cricket career, detailing his successes and failures and dovetailing them into a continuous written stream of encouraging himself into always thinking positively, was the appropriate man for Warne to confide in. He was appalled at Warne's negative attitude and geed him up. The words may have been trite to an outsider – be positive, confident, enjoy yourself – but they transformed Warne and he walked out onto the ground strangely self assured, like a man who knows he has nothing left to lose.

He bowled well but by the end of his eighth over had not taken a wicket. The West Indies were one wicket for 143 and proceeding at a pace and with a commanding bunch of wickets still in reserve that suggested they were going to win the game. Richie Richardson, nearing his half-century, was gradually getting on top of Warne's bowling, sensing that the leg spinner was tiring, and planning to belt him out of the attack. Richardson's contempt for Warne was profound. He had watched him try to bowl wrong'uns and flippers in the first innings and regarded them as having all the flair and danger of a spit ball thrown against a battleship.

Border kept Warne on for a ninth over and he bowled three regulation leg breaks, one of which Richardson smoothly stroked for four to bring up his half-century. It was at the top of his run-up preparing to bowl his fourth delivery that Warne began his career as a true Test cricketer. He could have played it safe by bowling a standard leg break, but instead he decided to bowl a flipper, a delivery he had failed to control in his five Test matches. At this stage of the innings, with his future as a Test cricketer at stake, one can only describe his decision as a mixture of courage, hope and desperation. If he failed and the ball was hit for a four or six, then he knew Richardson would begin to flay his bowling. If that happened, then his nascent Test career was all but finished. He would end up being used as a teasing example of someone who couldn't cut it at Test cricket level, just like Johnny Watkins.

He bowled again. Richardson saw the ball bounce on a length that looked like easy pickings for a swipe to the boundary. Then he had to abruptly change his mind because it was coming on to him much more quickly than he expected and was not bouncing. Then the ball seemed to be dying on him, like a balloon rapidly running out of air. He held his bat stiffly and played for the ball to deviate from right to left but it went straight on, sneaking in between his pads and an uncertain vertical bat and hitting the stumps. It was the perfect flipper, probably one of the best ever bowled. Richardson, his face partly hidden in the shadows cast by his hat (it had such a ludicrously wide brim that it resembled a burgundy-coloured flying saucer), looked up at Warne in momentary disbelief and then he strode off, incredulous at the way he had been bowled. Given his underestimation of Warne, he probably blamed a fault in the pitch.

No doubt in the West Indian dressing-room there was talk of bashing Warne the trundler out of the attack. For all their one and a half decades of continued success, West Indian batsmen had considered the idea of a leg spinner dominating them as unlikely as a sissy beating up a thug in the school ground. Not having the footwork to play spin, they decided either to belt the ball out of the ground in order to destroy Warne's confidence or with ponderous feet to poke at the ball as if trying to swish away a particularly annoying insect. Arthurton, the next batsman, chose the former route. He belted Warne and quickly had thirteen runs in thirteen balls, when he decided to inflict more damage on the spinner by charging him. He jumped out of his crease with all the blind alacrity of a World War I soldier leaping out of his trench. The ball drifted past his hapless swinging bat and Healy stumped him. Warne couldn't believe it. The wicket had been so easy. Arthurton had done most of the work for him. You could sense that he knew this would be his day. His eyes sparkled. A confident swagger became noticeable. And most importantly, the ball now felt a part of him. He knew where it would land, what it would do, and how much it would spin.

It was the beginning of a glorious afternoon for Warne. The confidence he gained in bowling the West Indian captain was obvious as he teased the batsmen with spin, drift and variations so subtle they were lost on his addled opponents who prodded at the deliveries or decided to go down fighting by attempting to whack the ball out of the ground. Australia won handsomely and Warne, having taken seven wickets, walked off the ground to a standing ovation from his home-town crowd and right into a media flurry that went on through the next day until the Cricket Board's media manager called a halt to it at Warne's insistence.

There was no doubt he liked the attention and

publicity, but even though he had won the match Warne was still prey to doubts. What if this were just a brief success and he was to return to the failures of the previous Tests? The ever-discourteous Richardson probably voiced some of the leg spinner's doubts when he remarked: 'He got seven wickets and bowled well. But I don't think he is a threat really.' Despite Border's public praise for Warne as a wonderful risk-taker, the spinner still felt out of his depth. The next Test confirmed his fears. In a rain-interrupted match he was taken to by the dazzling left-hander Brian Lara, who narrowly missed scoring a triple century. The swagger went, the cheeky smile too. In their place was constant lip licking, nervous massaging of the ball as he prepared to bowl, and that now-familiar expression in his eyes of desperate hope that the ball itself would do something unexpected, because he himself didn't believe he was capable of such a delivery. The next Test Warne again only took one wicket in a match that was one of the most thrilling ever, with the West Indies winning by only one run after dismissing Australia's last batsman, Craig McDermott. Border's hope of winning the Frank Worrell Trophy was ruined by one man, Curtly Ambrose, whose first innings attack on Australia in the Fifth Test was one of the most devastating in the history of Test cricket. His seven wickets for 25 runs (with all seven wickets taken for just one run) crushed Australia. Warne himself went wicketless. His inner fears were proven, his success in Melbourne had been an aberration.

Still, he was chosen for the tour of New Zealand and at the end of the three-match series he had taken

17 wickets at fifteen runs per wicket, an astonishing figure given his previous bowling average. He was also named man-of-the-series. Yet for those Australians sceptical about his talent all it proved was that the New Zealanders were shoddy players of leg spin. Those who hadn't seen his performances didn't realise how much he was improving his craft and just how impressed some of his opponents were. The splendid New Zealand batsman Martin Crowe thought Warne 'has the mark of a potentially great leg spin bowler'.

One of the people who had the highest regard for him was Allan Border who, in his determination to hold on to the Ashes, concocted a plan to give the English batsmen a false sense of security. He recognised that English cricketers and journalists knew little about Warne, except that he was a bit of a 'larrikin surfie' who had taken a few wickets but was nothing special. Border thought that three batsmen stood in the way of Australia winning the series, Graeme Hick, Graham Gooch and Michael Atherton, so when the Australians played Worcestershire in a lead-up game to the First Test, Border instructed Warne to bowl only leg breaks and not reveal his special deliveries. Hick had already asked the all-rounder Chris Cairns about Warne, and the New Zealander said his captain Martin Crowe was a great admirer but he himself thought Warne was a limited bowler with few variations. By the time Hick had belted Warne and raced to 187 he was in agreement with Cairns; Warne was a common bowler and would play no significant role in the Tests. For Warne, bowling under his captain's instructions, it was not only frustrating to allow himself to be hit around the ground and many times out of it, but also unsettling. His confidence was still brittle and the easy way Hick handled him unnerved him. The Ashes were the most important Test matches for Australians. As Warne has said, 'It is beaten into you as a youngster that you've got to beat the Poms.' After the savage assault on his bowling he was prey to many doubts. What if the other English batsmen took to him like Hick did? What if the English pitches didn't suit his spinners? What if his occasional successes so far were merely examples of luck and chance? Border probably didn't realise just how close his strategy came to destroying his leg spinner's confidence.

When the First Test began in early June, 1993, the English batsmen and media, following Hick's example, had dismissed Warne; he seemed as real a threat as his outrageously yellow hair was real blond. So when he came on to bowl his first ball, the batsmen waiting in the pavilion had little concern about him, given also the fact that the best English player of spin, Mike Gatting, was about to face him. The English press always liked to refer to Gatting as looking like an English bulldog, but really he looked like a plump surly barman. In contrast, Warne had never looked fitter. All he wanted to do with the first ball was to land it on length and gradually find his rhythm in the first couple of overs. He gripped the ball for a standard leg break and moved in to bowl with that deceptively casual stroll of his. The ball left his hand and from the moment it did, he could tell it was a good delivery as it curled from left to right like the amiable drift of a frisbee. It landed outside the leg stump and then, suddenly animated, jagged and jumped back the other way. Gatting hopefully prodded at the ball as it turned almost at right angles from right to left, but it whipped past his bat and hit off stump. It had turned some two or more feet. Warne jumped up and held his fist aloft. Gooch, standing at the bowler's end, could hardly believe what he saw. Gatting's reaction was of astonishment. The ball had spun so far that he thought the wicket-keeper might have accidentally hit the stumps. The Australians were celebrating but still Gatting stood there, perplexed and amazed at how far the ball had turned. The thought crossed his mind that it might have hit a stone. Merv Hughes, a wonderful fast bowler, who carried an enormous beer gut and wore a florid moustache that made him look like a villain in a Victorian melodrama, ran up to congratulate Warne and thought of telling the tardy Gatting to get off the ground, but the Englishman was now on his way, having stayed a good ten seconds after being initially too stupefied to move. Gatting's incredulous reaction would affect the rest of the English team: 'You couldn't imagine what it must have done to their rooms,' Hughes later wrote. 'Gatting was *the* player of spin and was there specifically to combat Warney.' Later that night a still-confounded Gatting asked Warne what had happened. 'You just missed a leg break, buddy,' replied Warne, but it was more than just a leg break, as everyone knew who saw it that day. It was as special a delivery as many had ever seen. There are some who say the best ball ever bowled in a Test was Fleetwood Smith's left-arm spinner that bowled the great Walter Hammond and won a Test match for Australia, but as far as the newspapers were concerned, Warne's was 'the ball of the century' and 'the best ball ever seen in cricket history'. Even now when Warne watches a replay he says he still gets 'tingles'. He cannot fully explain the beauty of the delivery to himself. He variously calls it an accident or 'It was the Bloke Upstairs saying it was meant to happen'. Perhaps it was a combination of all these things. It seems that Warne, like all great sportsmen, has an in-built sense of occasion. It was his first ball in Ashes cricket, it was in England, the home of cricket, and was delivered to the best English player of spin. To see a perplexed and stunned Gatting unable to move as he tried to figure out what had happened only added to the drama. Gatting had the look of a man who had been conned out of a fortune and still didn't know how the trickery occurred.

But to prove it was no fluke, Warne's first ball of his next over spun almost as much and Robin Smith helplessly edged the ball to be caught in slips. Too late the English side realised they had been duped. Border had initiated the hustle. The new young kid on the block had hoodwinked them. Warne's first ball in the Test was so unexpected and so extraordinary that the English batsmen, as Warne himself recognised, never recovered psychologically from it. That single ball was to dramatically change Warne's life forever.

5: The Golden Boy

The momentary and occasional bouts of media hype Warne had experienced up until now were nothing to what he was about to undergo. Newspapers, especially the tabloids, were obsessed by him. Warne was a godsend. Unlike the crabby, taciturn captain, Allan Border, or the fast bowler Merv Hughes, whose slapstick pranks, fart jokes and unathletic body made him laughable when he wasn't threatening, Warne confirmed the stereotypical image the English now had of Australians. Instead of picturing the typical Australian as a laconic shearer or sportsman, the English now envisaged a different sort of Australian. The English had taken to several Australian television soap operas with a voracity that seemed to some Australian commentators to be quite inexplicable. A particular favourite was *Neighbours*. It was only when I was in a working-class London bar one miserable winter that I realised just how appealing the shows were to the English. The whole bar went silent when two popular Australian soap operas appeared one after the other on a small television set in the corner next to a clothes rack that held dismal damp coats and a motley collection of old and stained scarves. I had never seen the programs back in Australia for the very reasons I now noticed – they were corny, the story-lines trite and the acting shallow, yet compared to the grey and dour soap operas the English were used to, they had a carefree ebullience, infectious optimism and were bathed in bright Australian sunlight. The Australia of *Neighbours* was an endless suburbia of enormous front lawns, crimeless streets, cuddly labradors, carefree chil- dren, a swimming pool in every backyard and, instead of problems of life and death, the essential story-lines were of average day-to-day problems of waiting for the plumber or questioning whether the daughter was too young to go out on a first date, of comically exasperated parents and young lovers rushing to the altar before they had rushed into bed with each other. It was always sunny and the size of the houses and the casual affluence was appealing, especially to the English who had endured Margaret Thatcher's austere and relentless eco- nomic reforms. There were few ethnics in the show and there was nothing that couldn't be solved over a cup of tea. *Neighbours* was a portrait of white Australia as a gated and happily carefree suburban community, and surpris- ingly similar to the world Warne grew up in. Academic Alan Mckee, author of *Australian Television: a Genealogy of Great Moments*, says of the soap opera: 'The worst thing that happens in *Neighbours* is that somebody's pet mouse escapes. No-one has HIV, nobody is raped, nobody has to deal with anything particularly traumatic

or disturbing.' Hundreds of British tourists still visit the
Neighbours outdoor set every week.

The two major stars of the show confirmed its good-
natured and benign atmosphere. Kylie Minogue's
character was a chirpy, optimistic girl, with a mass of
golden curls and an unthreatening asexual appeal, and
her co-star, the handsome blond Jason Donovan, had an
uncomplicated and enthusiastic outlook on life. Both
stars embodied the appeal of *Neighbours*. Australians
were optimists, straightforward and surprisingly moral.
Unlike the English, Australians had limitless futures
which were always going to be rosy and comfortable
and awfully nice.

Shane Warne's popularity in England had a lot to do
with this image. For a British journalist like Alan Lee,
Warne was 'a boy off the beaches, bleached and bronzed
as if auditioning for *Neighbours*.' Warne was himself a fan
of the show and on his previous trip to England had
made a scurrilous and since destroyed video with mate
Rick Gough that parodied the show. Warne's artlessness
and lack of guile seemed very familar to those millions
of viewers who were fans of the show and especially of
Kylie and Jason, as they were known. Warne also had a
girlfriend who was blonde and attractive, in a way
almost Warne's mirror image, and she too could have
auditioned for *Neighbours*. He had met the 23-year-old
Simone Callahan back in Australia and she impressed his
friends and journalists as a rather no-nonsense, sensible
young woman (character traits which would have to
hold her in good stead during the bumpy ride of the
next decade). Warne was smitten with her and after

the First Test found himself proposing when they were rowing across Lake Windermere in the Lake District: 'There was nothing premeditated about it, even though from our first weeks together I knew that she was the right girl for me.'

Such placid moments off the field were seldom. Every time he opened a newspaper there were stories about him. Old girlfriends were interviewed and Warne was astonished at how much the tabloids wrote about him was fabricated. He had now entered the world of the celebrity where there is the narcissistic thrill of seeing yourself everywhere, even though you are portrayed in such an exaggerated fashion that you resemble images in funhouse mirrors more than any genuine reflection. Privacy had been easy to find in the anonymity of failure, but success meant it was a thing of the past. Warne complained that he couldn't even sit down for a meal without someone thrusting a piece of paper in front of him for an autograph. He was quickly learning what Kylie Minogue and Jason Donovan had previously discovered. The tabloid press can be voracious and reckless with the truth. The media infatuation was astonishing to him: 'The whole world seemed to want to know everything about me on and off the field. People wanted to know how I spent my spare time and, more important it seemed, with whom … one newspaper published a list entitled "The Things you never knew about Shane Warne" – and I swear I didn't know five of them myself.' In the 1930s Don Bradman withdrew into himself and his marriage in order to escape such adulation. The only recent comparison for Warne was Dennis Lillee, but the fast bowler had kept his equilibrium by deliberately removing himself from the public gaze, and as he lived in Perth that had made it easier. But Warne liked the adulation. Less than a year ago he had been playing for his cricket life in Sri Lanka and every time he had gone out to bowl his cricket future had been at stake. Now he was the Golden Boy. Sponsors descended on him because, as one executive was to say, 'He's a good regular guy. He doesn't big-note. He's great to do business with.' There were so many potential sponsors that his manager was overwhelmed. He was given a column to write or at least he had given his name to it. Nothing like this had happened to an Australian cricketer for a long time.

Amidst this hullabaloo his team-mates were worried that Warne might be sucked into the vortex of media fame and spend too much time on such things as product endorsement, but in a way, Warne was more prepared than they knew. Unlike Byron, who had woken one morning to find he was famous, Warne's rise had been gradual and erratic and he knew what it was to fail abysmally and publicly. He had been a hero for an occasional Test and then had spent the next Tests bowling so badly that he was afraid of being dropped. He was so unsure of his consistency that originally he expected to play only a couple of Test matches in the Ashes series. His team-mates were slow to understand that what goaded Warne was his desire to succeed. Beneath the affable and boofhead exterior he presents to the public is a man with an incandescent will to win and to prove himself, both to the public and his peers. He found it difficult to be rejected by the public, whose attitude, he was to discover, was refracted increasingly through the prism of constantly carping journalists with their sanctimonious moralism, but he was downright distressed if he thought he had let down his team-mates. Frequently and honestly he has said that to win a man-of-the-match award means nothing to him if the team hasn't won, and television cameras frequently have picked out that hollow expression of thanks when he has received an award after the team has lost. Even though the English media lauded him, he was still to convince himself that he was good enough. The press compared him to such great spinners as Clarrie Grimmett and O'Reilly and the comparison genuinely embarrassed and bothered him. But he was motivated to try to be worthy of the overheated acclaim he was getting.

He took eight wickets in the First Test and then another eight in the second. It was not only the number of wickets he was getting that made him news, but the way in which he took them. He prided himself in never buying a wicket by throwing up bad balls in the hope that a batsman would hit a catch. His method was to attack the batsmen with a tremendously turning ball or deliveries of such peerless variation that he utterly bewildered his opponents. He dismissed Alec Stewart with a ball he called the 'zooter', one that floats out of the front of the fingers and goes straight on off the pitch. Then there was his unorthodox method of bowling around the wicket. The shoulder is placed under more pressure and the bowler has to be relentlessly accurate. If the ball doesn't pitch in the right place it is easy for the batsman to swing it to the boundary on the leg side. Warne aimed for the footmarks left by the right-armed fast bowlers and in hitting them could turn the ball prodigiously. Because he bowled two tail enders with the ploy, the wickets went unrecognised for the exceptional deliveries they were. Gaining confidence with each Test match Warne began to develop as a strategist. He could now afford to experiment. The English were too unsure to attack him by using their feet to get to the pitch of the ball and they seemed resigned to staying at the crease, as if their feet were weighed down by the lead of fear and apprehension.

If any wicket indicated just how far he had pro-gressed on the tour then it was that of Graham Gooch. Warne admired the English batsman, an unpretentious, mustachioed man whose mental toughness was leg-endary but occasionally brittle. Warne respectfully called him 'Mr Gooch' but his competitiveness was flourishing and he decided he not only wanted to get his wicket but in a manner that was counter to the prevailing ortho-doxy. Warne had noticed that Gooch played his deliveries rather casually when they pitched on leg stump. In the Fifth Test at Edgbaston in Birmingham Warne told the bemused Border that he had a plan to get Gooch out. Much to the captain's astonishment it worked. The ball he proceeded to bowl was, in a way, superior to the so-called 'ball of the century'. Warne came around the wicket and the ball floated down the leg side so far from the stumps that it could have been called a wide. Gooch dismissively and casually thrust a pad out just in case it turned in, but it was done without any conviction. The ball landed and then jumped laterally (or as commentators like to say of some of Warne's special deliveries 'spat and jumped like a cobra'), curved behind Gooch's legs and hit the wicket. Like many batsmen since, Gooch was startled to hear the ball hit his stumps. Surely there had been a mistake? He briefly turned, saw the three stumps lurching at different angles, and knew by the delirious pogo dance of the wicket-keeper that Warne had conjured an almost miraculous delivery.

As Warne's strategic confidence grew so did his belief that he belonged in the team. And in the fashion of Australian cricket since Ian Chappell's team which had revelled in abusing opponents to earn the tag of the 'Ugly Australians', so Warne, now one of the boys and a great admirer of Merv Hughes's constant sledging of the opposition, took to sledging himself. He sent off the Welshman Matthew Maynard with, 'Take that fucking shot back to Wales.'

Warne bowled beautifully throughout the Ashes tour. But his contribution was more than the number of wickets he took. Border was beginning to understand that Warne was transforming the game. Not only was a contemporary team becoming reliant on a spinner rather than a pace attack but the placid wait for a wicket which seemed to be a huge part of the spinner's trade was no more. Warne was capable of taking a wicket every time he walked in to bowl. His aggression, massive turn and growing tactical nous meant that Border had to actively support the spinner by setting attacking fields that would have alarmed less-accomplished spinners, who relied on defensive outfielders. For Border it meant that, given the quickness of Warne's over-rate and his potential to get a wicket every ball, a captain had to be always thinking, always aggressive, always tactically prepared. With a fast bowler a captain and fieldsmen can relax between deliveries but Warne's short run-up, quick over-rate and relentless and ruthless probing of the batsman meant that this was not possible. Like the bowler, the captain and fieldsmen had to enter a higher state of concentration and anticipation. Yes, there had been excellent leg spinners before, but that had been decades ago and since then it was thought that the days of a leg spinner winning matches was over.

His sheer skill entranced everyone and, what was to become a common feature of his career, spectators at the game or viewers watching television would suddenly go quiet when Warne came into bowl. He was a man who was indeed like a conjurer and his beguiling of the batsmen and the many variations of deception he practised were enthralling. Test cricket was no longer just the brutish fast bowler and the cowering or courageous batsman and the long wait between balls. Now it was a matter of craft, expertise, deception and the patient setting-up of a batsman. (How often in his career did commentators refer to Warne as the spider patiently weaving his web to capture his prey?) So remarkable was his bowling that even English cricket writers were hoping his career wouldn't be blighted by injury because they adored seeing him bowl.

The 1993 Ashes tour was one of the highlights of Warne's life. It had been only a year since he had played in Sri Lanka but now he was crucial to the team's success. The aimless and drifting life he had found himself falling into after his football career finished before it even started was over. During that English summer he had found a sense of perfection and purpose on those soft green ovals. The pitch of twenty-two yards was no longer a fraught and ominous place. Over the six Tests he had claimed the twenty-two yards as his territory and it was now up to batsmen to earn their place on it. Outside the boundary ropes he was the media's darling and eager sponsors flocked to him. The future seemed bright and golden.

6: Bowled, Shane

Warne's success and charisma were having an enormous effect on the number of spectators coming to the grounds and those viewing the Tests on television. Boys gave up fast bowling and took up leg spinning. He had taken a near-forgotten cricket art and reconstituted it as not only something glamorous but also something that mentally unhinged batsmen. You needed to look no further than the South African Daryll Cullinan to see what Warne was capable of doing to a man's psyche. Cullinan came to Australia for the 1993–94 three-match Test series. Cullinan was regarded as one of the brightest talents to emerge in South African cricket, and, boy, did he know it too. He was cocky, young and gifted, a volatile mix at any time. Awed by his own reputation, he sledged Australian cricketers with all the theatrical bile of a veteran. This annoyed the Australians greatly, especially Warne, who has been consistent in his attitude that you are not entitled to arrogance if you haven't proved yourself on the field. (Paul Adams, the South African spinner whose bowling action is like an acrobat caught in a cyclone, was to earn Warne's ire a few years later by his arrogant backchat and insolent tomfoolery when first playing against the Australians.) Warne has always thought that he earned his place in the Australian team and in doing so earned the right to be cocky and confident.

Cullinan's backchat was not matched by his early performances in Australia. In the First Test Warne bowled him with a splendid flipper and as the South African walked off Warne abused him mightily. Over the years Cullinan's confidence was eroded by Warne's almost clinical dissection of his technique and confidence. Warne had his measure, especially with the flipper, which the South African found almost impossible to pick. As David Boon has written: 'From that moment [Warne's first dismissal of the South African] on, as Warney cast his spell around him, Cullinan would be greeted with: "Is the shower already running, Daryll?" More than most, Cullinan suffered from Shane's flipper. "It's going to be the third ball, Daryll," we'd tell him. "Make sure you come forward. Oh, you're out!"'

Warne went even further. He began to publicly brag that Cullinan was his bunny and, after a match, made deliberately inflammatory remarks like: 'I don't care how many I get, so long as I get Cullinan.' The more Cullinan tried to counter-attack, the more ignominious were his batting failures. Even on his thirtieth birthday there was no respite as Warne took his wicket again. Here was a gifted batsman whose batting average was around 44 against all other countries except Australia where it was a dismal 12 runs. Cullinan was so mentally tortured by Warne that he sought professional psychological help. Just before the 1997–98 tour of Australia a newspaper revealed that the South African had been to a psychiatrist to overcome the leg spinner. Warne was incredulous: 'I knew Daryll was a bit fragile at times, but never imagined he would go to a shrink to learn how to read a googly.' This was all Warne needed to know in order to finally rid himself of a batsman whose early arrogance was built around a thick carapace of confidence in his own talents but whose self-belief was now as thin and brittle as an eggshell. So when Cullinan took strike for his first ball Warne said to him: 'Daryll, I've waited so long for this moment and I'm going to send you back to that leather couch.' A few balls later, Cullinan was bowled for a duck and left the ground a man whose confidence was as barren as a saltpan. Realising that Cullinan had been psychologically crushed by the spinner, the South African selectors dropped him for the rest of the series. When Australia played in South Africa in early 1997 Warne waited impatiently to bowl at his patsy, telling Mark Waugh, as Cullinan came out to bat, 'I'm going to have this bloke for breakfast.' Warne was as good as his word and, after struggling for ten balls, Cullinan was out without scoring. Not content to keep his mental domination of Cullinan to the cricket paddock, he told the press that, 'All I wanted in this game was [to get] Daryll Cullinan. I wanted to make sure those old [psychological] scars don't heal too quick.' Despite again batting well against other countries Cullinan was dropped from the South African 2001–02 touring party. The selectors reasoned that Cullinan was not mentally fit to face up to Warne and to see the leg spinner crush him would be too demoralising for the rest of the team that was hoping (a futile hope as it turned out) to defeat Australia and become the world's number one team. Cullinan was never to face Warne again in a Test match. Warne's verbal assaults both on the field and in the media had taken their toll on the South African, who in 1997 said of him: 'If you're going to use gamesmanship, fine, but if you're going to over-step that mark, it can be dangerous and it can get nasty. I respect him tremendously as a cricketer, but I don't know how much respect I have for him as a person.' Four years later he was more generous (perhaps the therapy had helped), and he said of Warne: 'Without doubt he is the best bowler I've faced. It's his variation, his consistency and through the years he hasn't bowled many bad balls. He's an awesome bowler. I tried to prove that wrong but to my downfall I found out it was true.'

This brutal and ruthless dominance reveals a side to Warne that is seldom commented on. He couldn't phys-ically intimidate the batsmen but he could play on and prey on their doubts and toy with their self-belief. His career has shown that Test cricket is mostly a mental game. Test cricketers have ability or else they wouldn't be chosen, but it is how they deal with stress and doubt that distinguishes the average from the great. The game may appear to be staid and even genial but it is a sport where a moment of doubt can destroy you and once an opponent senses that doubt or wavering self-belief then it is ruthlessly exploited. I was reminded of this when I was playing cricket against a team that had a leg spinner who had once been part of the New South Wales cricket squad. He was a quiet, unassuming man and I watched him from the safety of the non-striker's end bowl an over of exquisite leg spin against a team-mate who could barely get bat onto ball and was finally put out of his misery by a perfect leg break that took his middle stump. I congratulated the bowler, but all he did was shake his head as if it meant little. Afterwards I learned from one of his team-mates that he had been one of the most promising leg spinners many had seen, but a Test cricketer took to him in a club game and he lost all rhythm, confidence and self-belief. His confidence shattered, all he was capable of doing afterwards was playing social cricket where his fragile but wonderful talent was wasted. It was not unlike seeing a potential Chess Grand Master who had been mentally squashed by an opponent playing pickup games in the park. After you have reached the élite level many a battle is not so much with your opponent but with yourself. There is a constant oscillation that attempts to balance doubt and ego, blame and praise, and hesitation and resolve.

In the Test series against South Africa in 1994 Warne found that he had to draw on inner resources of self-control, which he discovered were more shallow than he realised. Everything had gone his way since the 1993 Ashes. The crowds, even the English ones, had been supportive and appreciative but in Australia's first tour of South Africa since the end of apartheid he was to find himself, like most of the Australian team, surrounded by some of the most boorish and unpleasant crowds he had ever faced. Players were spat on, oranges were thrown at them, and the crowds loudly chanted *'Warne's a Wanker'*. His new, gingerish goatee was also made fun of. It may be easy to block out constant noise and chants until they become an acoustic blur, but the threat of being spat upon or hit by oranges or other objects eats away at one's concentration. The cricket oval becomes not just a contest between bat and ball but something more ugly and venomous, like bear-baiting rinks where mastiffs were let loose on chained-up bears. There is little enjoyment. The crowd is silent and sullen if their team is losing and cockily offensive if winning. And, just as Warne himself mentally overwhelmed his patsy, Culli- nan, so the crowds, plus the deliberate phone calls waking him at all hours of the morning, began to affect him. His run-up, once relaxed and effortless, began to stiffen, as if he were a coiled spring of anger. He began to lose his loop and drift, sacrificing it to flat trajectory, vicious turn, and bounce. The cheerful, charming bloke was replaced by a snarling, grim-faced man. Team-mates knew he was testy and irritated with the crowds but they didn't know the depths of Warne's indignation. Once loved, he was now hated. Nothing could hurt him more. Retrospectively he called himself 'a time bomb waiting to explode'. In the second innings of the First Test match Warne was introduced into the attack and immediately took the wicket of the benign opener Andrew Hudson. What happened next stunned the leg spinner's team-mates because he rushed at Hudson, snarling and furious, yelling obscenities at him, telling him to 'Fuck off!, Fuck off outta here!' The astonished

Hudson could only look back at Healy grabbing Warne and pulling him away. 'I got the shock of my life,' Healy later wrote, 'and even had to physically restrain Warney from getting too close to the batsman.' Warne's face was screwed up in torment and a rage so primal that it's seldom seen except inside the boxing ring as in the famous photographs of Mohammed Ali's triumphant primate snarl as he stands over a supine, beaten opponent. He had snapped.

Warne is still astounded, even horrified by his own behaviour and the expression on his face that day: 'I look back at the [video]. I look an angry man. It's like I'm back playing football.' But he also recognised something else, 'I got a bit cocky and arrogant. I did a couple of things in South Africa I'm ashamed of when I sledged Andrew Hudson.' Admonished by Border, mortified by his own behaviour he went into the South African rooms and apologised. Praise, conceit, adulation, arrogance, the constant taunting chants, the many placards that spelt out in big letters things like 'Warne's mother is a goat' and 'It's not over until the Fat Boy Spins', the mocking press, had all been caught up in a tumultuous mental whirlpool churned up by the crowd's palpable and vicious desire to see him fail. In this maelstrom a dark self had briefly emerged and he didn't like what he saw. Warne didn't have and never would have the mental resources to confront that side of himself. It frightened him. He knew he had to make a conscious decision to never lose it again. But he wasn't allowed to forget it. He had to deal with the consequences of his actions and fame.

The incident was broadcast on Australian television with another one of an irate Hughes belligerently waving a bat as a weapon at a spectator who had spat on him. For both incidents Warne and Hughes were fined by the match referee, but the Australian media wanted more. Newspaper editorials and radio shock jocks demanded they be banned from Test cricket and sent back to Australia. Commentators said they were ashamed to be Australian and Warne was a disgrace. It was the first time that Warne realised just how fierce, implacable and self-righteous the media could be. An incident that he thought would go no further than the changing rooms where he apologised to Hudson now was blown out of all proportion. A grumbling media had to content itself with the Australian Cricket Board's decision to fine both Victorians their match fees. The ACB had been embarrassed into the decision by the press and their own policy of opposing sledging.

Warne, now irritated by the ACB's decision and the predatory media, shaved off his trendy but silly goatee (there is no room for retro beatniks on the conservative cricket paddock) and listened to the advice of his father who had just arrived and that of the vice-captain, Mark Taylor. His anger dissipated and he bowled well for the next two Test matches, but as far as the once-adoring public was concerned 'the halo' had slipped and was now a vigilante's noose around his neck. It was confirmation that underneath his casual larrikin exterior was just another Boofhead or Ugly Australian. It was the first indication Warne received that people's attitude to him was changing and that the media's love would be fickle and its intense interest in him would have its darker side. Sometimes he would find that he could do no right. He developed a mistrust of newspaper journalists, not an uncommon attitude with Test cricketers, whose suspicions of the press can verge on the paranoiac. Frances Edmonds, the wife of the English cricketer, Phil Edmonds, intimately knows about this tense relationship between journalists and cricketers, and in her entertaining book *Another Bloody Tour* writes: 'Unfortunately, [reporting on cricket] is sometimes a job which can be inimical to the criteria of an intimate friendship. Journalists are often obliged to write harsh, objective and fairly *ad hominem* criticism and some of the mega-egos … find even the vaguest hint of opprobrium difficult to stomach.' If this relationship with good reporters is uneasy then the relationships between players and the tabloids is distinctly frosty or with what Edmonds calls 'the filth dredgers and the roving columnists who rock in for a couple of days, gain a few superficial impressions and rock off to file a pile of inflammatory copy from a very safe distance'.

Roland Fishman tells of how the NSW team developed a system to protect its young players from journalists that couldn't be trusted, and who became known as 'coats'. 'If a young player was seen talking to a coat, a senior player would attract the player's attention and surreptitiously pull at his lapel, to indicate that the journalist was a coat.' Some journalists resent this exclusion greatly and find the players' studied indifference to them and preference for the company of their team-mates a sign of their aloofness and selfishness. Warne has been criticised for this. No matter how much time he has tried to give to the media it is still not enough. He is a man who finds it difficult to divide up his time efficiently, and his casual approach to returning reporters' calls became another cause for their criticism. As time went on he was to find that as far as the media were concerned there was no separation between his public and private life. Everything came in for scrutiny and criticism. There was the standard journalistic ploy of concocting stories out of nothing. When he celebrated the birth of his first child, Brooke, by smoking a cigar, a member of the Anti-Cancer Council, Judith Watt, was interviewed for her reaction and she promptly gave the prim, wowser answer the journalist wanted: 'It's such a shame that smoking is still deemed to be a symbol of success,' she opined and, of course, added the kicker, 'Cigar smokers have a two-and-a-half higher rate of lung cancer.' After a marvellous display of spin bowling against England at Old Trafford in 1997 Warne danced around the players' balcony swigging from a bottle of champagne and giving a one-finger salute to the mostly obnoxious crowd. Warne himself had no regrets: 'I carried on like a pork chop and really let my hair down. Some people like me, some people don't. I'm not going to lose any sleep about it.' The English saw it for what it was, as David Hopps wrote: 'Warne could do with some instructions in the Royal Wave. He has soaked up the crowd's baiting all summer in good humour, so during Australia's victory celebration he sticks out his stomach, gives it a hearty pat, and follows up with a lighthearted one-finger salute. This is presented in at least one tabloid dreamworld as poor sportsmanship.'

But for moralistic fury nothing can beat the contemporary Australian press. Cricket writers and columnists were outraged, and moralistic tirades were written about Warne damaging Australian cricket and how he should be ashamed of himself. After the Fifth Test match in the same series an exuberant Warne again celebrated on the players' balcony by doing a hip-swinging dance, a cricket stump in both hands raised above his head. Again, he was stung by a hail of hostile opinion probably best summed up by the pompous *Age* columnist Patrick Smith: 'Shane Warne has made a goose of himself. Again. Swaying on the balcony out-side the players' room, waving a stump high above his head. He then appeared to give the crowd the thumb as he left. His provocation and immature actions have sul-lied a fine victory.' A bewildered Warne could only write: 'Photographs confirm from the look in my eyes that I didn't mean anything nasty or provocative … Surely we are allowed to show a little emotion after winning the Ashes.' But Warne was learning there is nothing as shrill and incoherent as the sermons of columnists and sports writers.

After the South African tour he had a prolonged rest before a quick one-day competition in Sri Lanka and a tour of Pakistan. The new captain, Mark Taylor, realised that Warne was in danger of being over-bowled. He was developing minor, niggling injuries and had to be used as less of a workhorse than he had become under Border's leadership. And it was important that Warne be fully fit, because Taylor and his team were desperate to beat Pakistan and prove that the Australians could win on the subcontinent. Pakistan cricket teams have always been a collection of brilliant individuals rather than a cohesive unit, which seems to explain Pakistan's mercurial performances, ranging from the extraordinary to the dismal from one day to the next.

During the First Test against Pakistan in Karachi in October, 1994, Australia was playing well and the home team was set 314 runs to win. By the end of the fourth day the game was in the balance with Pakistan three wickets down for 157. Later that evening Warne picked up the phone in his hotel room which he was sharing with the off spinner Tim May, and was surprised to hear the Pakistani captain, Salim Malik, on the other end. This was unusual as Malik was an unpleasant, aloof man with a face disturbingly like a rodent, hence his nickname, 'The Rat'. Malik invited Warne and May to his room for what he said would be 'an interesting chat'. But May was too tired and Warne went alone. After some inconsequential talk about the close and intense match Malik said, 'You know, we cannot lose.' Warne laughed, believing that Malik was merely being cocky, but then the Pakistani repeated the statement, 'You don't understand. We cannot lose.' When he said it for a third time it gradually dawned on Warne that the Pakistani captain was hinting at something. Malik, exasperated by the Australian's obtuseness, then made an unmistakable offer: Warne and May would receive $200,000 in cash before midnight if they performed as instructed the following day. Warne was stunned, but Malik, surprisingly confident, told the Australian that if he and May bowled well outside the off stump then the game would be a draw. 'Are you kidding?' was all Warne could say, but the Pakistani wasn't. Warne said he wouldn't be part of it and before leaving told Malik to 'get stuffed'. He returned to his room and told his room-mate what had happened. At first May treated it as a joke, but once he grasped the seriousness of Malik's offer he realised there had probably been a huge betting plunge on either a Pakistan victory or a draw. May told Warne to tell the Rat to get fucked. Warne rang Malik and dutifully passed on his friend's obscenity and added that Australia was going to beat Pakistan.

The next day was as intensely fought a match as any Warne had been involved in. Just when it seemed as though Australia would win the last pair put on a 53-run partnership and needed only three runs to win when Warne came in to bowl. In a daring move Taylor and Warne decided to leave a great part of the on side vacant to tempt Inzamam to hit in that area. The plan worked beautifully up to a point. The Pakistani tried to hit the ball into the vacant area and missed it, the ball bounced low and passed by the off stump with the hefty and notoriously slow Inzamam out of his crease. But Healy, normally the safest of wicket-keepers, failed to gather in the ball to make the stumping before Inzamam could get back to the safety of his crease and it raced past him to the boundary. Pakistan had won by one wicket. After a devastated Warne collected his man-of-the-match trophy, a sardonic Malik walked past him, telling him he was stupid not to have taken the money, given that Australia had lost. Warne felt insulted and, as he says, 'I wanted to nail him there and then with the old knuckle sandwich.' The buoyant Pakistani captain also approached David Boon at the presentation ceremony, with a nudge, nudge, wink, wink, offer of hashish.

What never occurred to Warne is why Salim Malik was so confident and brash in approaching him in the first place. A couple of years later he would realise the reason when the tour, which had originated in Sri Lanka, would come back to haunt him, just as the smarmy Salim Malik haunted him in the following two Tests. It seemed unfair to Warne but the corrupt Pakistani had his measure on the cricket field. Warne bowled exceptionally well but Malik scored heavily, mocking the Australian as someone who had a limited variety of deliveries, all three of which he found absurdly easy to pick. Even the Australian fieldsmen hissing 'Cheat, cheat' didn't disturb him.

After the enervating and disappointing tour of Pakistan, where Australia lost the series, it was with some relief that Warne turned his attention to the English tour of Australia in 1994–95. The English team was so threatened by the Australian spinner that the players spent hours watching a compilation tape of Warne taking wickets against them during the previous tour. When Warne found out he was amazed at the curious psychology of their approach. Countless viewings of him taking wickets made him seem invincible. And yet even the South African coaches and teams were to spend an inordinate amount of time studying videos of Warne, trying to analyse his bowling and penetrate its mysteries, a process fraught with problems, as cricket coach Steve Rixon said of the 2001–02 South African team: 'They have to be careful about overload. Because Warne is a problem for them, they can take it to the nth degree, looking at video after video, but then it can become too much and they start to see things that aren't there.'

The transfixed Englishmen during the 1994–95 tour were no closer to understanding Warne's deliveries than before. He took twenty wickets and in the first two Tests a succession of batsmen with dreamy, doomed expressions came and went, in what seemed like an abruptly edited montage of fleeting appearances. In the first match he produced one of his most perfect deliveries, a superb flipper that made the batsman, Alec Stewart, almost cry out in frustration and exasperation at having been comprehensively fooled. Determined to finally work out the leg spinner's secrets, Stewart and his captain, Michael Atherton, sat up in the back of the grandstand watching Warne bowling to their teammates, hoping that everything would be made plain through the magnification of a pair of binoculars. The television cameras caught them in the act and made them seem inept and comical in their inability to deal with the spinner. For some English reporters it seemed that England were playing not Australia but Warne. His dominance continued in the Second Test where he got the hat-trick he had just missed in the previous one. Even Alec Stewart, at the non-striker's end, told Warne when, after consecutive wickets, Devon Malcolm walked out to bat, 'You'll never have a better chance of getting a hat-trick.' Deciding not to waste a fancy ball on the tail end batsman as he had done against Tufnell, his intended hat-trick victim in the previous Test, Warne bowled a bouncy leg break which hit Malcolm on the gloves. The ball jumped out onto the leg side where David Boon, amazingly athletic for a man who resembles a beer keg firmly balanced on two tree stumps, dived to take a neat catch just before it hit the ground. Warne appeared so indomitable that in the future the English captain tried to make sure that Warne never got to bowl against them in the last innings. On a five-day-old pitch that had crumbled with wear and tear the leg spinner was unplayable.

After the first two Tests Warne was back in favour with the media. He was called Wizard, Genius, Beguiling, and a Magician. He was dubbed 'The Sultan of Spin' and 'The Sheik of Tweak'. Channel Nine began to groom him for an eventual spot as a commentator after he retired. As the cricket commentator Tony Greig says: 'On Channel Nine we really sell cricket hard. We really get behind good players, so much so that we turn them into millionaires. We don't hold back at all. If someone's good, boy, we unashamedly make 'em the best in the world.' Warne's relationship with television was symbiotic. It found him telegenic and he in turn began to learn from it. Even more so than, say, Dennis Lillee, Warne is a product of the television age and the way it televised cricket. After the Packer revolution, when the mogul founded World Series Cricket, the game would never be the staid affair it once was. Now that commercial television was interested in Test cricket, the former bland coverage of the ABC or the BBC had to trans-

mute into something continually exciting or else alien-
ate their commercial viewers, whose patience was
limited, and whose taste was more inclined towards the
heightened spectacle of one-day cricket.

Channel Nine developed the concept of narratives.
There was the overall story of the five-day game but
within that came several narratives within narratives.
After each ball was bowled it was shown in slow motion
and analysed while the bowler prepared to bowl the
next ball. There was not only the study of what the ball
had done and how the batsman had reacted but the
developing story of the battle between the individual
bowler and batsman, so that even if a game looked like
becoming a tame draw, the commentators could ignore
this and concentrate on the battles between individuals.
Warne provided the extra dimension of analysing the
extraordinary, lapidary complexity and range of his
bowling and examining the fierce psychological battles
with his opponents. If the quick bowlers were made to
seem like boxers delivering punches, Warne was made
to seem like a chess grand master or a Grand Inquisitor
constantly probing for suspect thoughts and fragile
defences. With close-ups and slow motion these battles
took on a singular quality, as if they were narrative sub-
plots. Warne may have occasionally become exasperated
with the intrusive microphones on the pitch, which
picked up sledging and the slow-motion close-ups,
which made it all too obvious he was shouting obscenities (and even in 2002, after years of realising the
cameras seldom missed anything, there were still many
viewers complaining that it was all too easy to read his

lips), but he was learning from television how to con-
struct his own narrative for the benefit of both the
opponent and the viewer. He began to dramatise his
bowling. There was a much more studied pause at the
top of his run, as if he were seriously deciding what
magic he was going to conjure up. The few seemingly
amiable steps of his run-up, the tongue poking out and
the grunt of effort, became trademarks as did his rueful
pause if the ball failed to get a wicket. At such times he
sagaciously stroked his chin as if to say, even if the ball
had been hit for a four, *Boy, you were lucky*. He developed
a windmill swing of his arms that finished with a punch
in the air when he had taken a wicket. His bowling took
on the added flavour of a performance and occasionally
culminated in doffing his hat and bowing to the
applauding crowd. The cricket oval became his stage.
He was the star performer and the Master of Illusion.
He knew how he looked on television. He understood
the power of the close-up and the potency of the slow-
motion replay, and created his *persona* accordingly. At
times the exaggerated chin-stroking or the windmill
spin of arms that ended with a finger duplicating an
umpire giving a batsman out had the aura of parody
about it (underscored by the mechanically repetitive and
monotonous strine cry of 'Bowled, Shane' or 'Bowled,
Warnie' coming from Healy behind the stumps). It was
no wonder that since his early days he was nicknamed
'Hollywood', because not only did he like to bask in the
warm glow of the media's interest in him, he also knew
how to play to the viewing public. The more he performed, the more television took to him. The media's

fascination with him helped him to psychologically overwhelm a new opponent who had heard about his genius and had probably seen him on endless replays. Because of cable and satellite television, anyone who was interested could watch a Test match being played anywhere in the world. Warne became more than a cricket player, he became a contemporary legend. By the time a player faced Warne for the first time his brain had long been saturated with the legend of the Australian's genius. It's probably true to say that Warne's high profile, raised to dizzying heights by flattering television images, created such uncertainty and defen-siveness in some batsmen that their dismissal was more due to his aura than the reality of his bowling. As South African wicket-keeper Dave Richardson commented: 'The Australian media builds [the players] up the best. Eventually you are seeing Shane Warne's googly spinning a metre.' He had become both a bowl-ing genius and a grand performer.

7: The Spirit is Strong, the Flesh is Weak

By the time he was twenty-six Warne's body was starting to develop frustrating and persistent injuries. The constant bowling in Tests and one-day cricket was taking its toll. His shoulder was sore, but the most pressing problem was his spinning finger. During the World Cup in 1996, which Australia lost to the Sri Lankans, the finger was causing him excruciating pain every time he bowled. He was given cortisone injections into the knuckle but the pain grew worse. When his physiotherapist was massaging Warne's forearm his fingers would twitch and spasm uncontrollably. His leg break could no longer spin as far as before and some of his other variations, like the flipper and the zooter, were impossibly painful to bowl. Warne kept putting off the operation on his finger. Former players and even specialists thought that the complete rehabilitation of his finger after an operation might be impossible. In all likelihood the finger would remain stiff and make it

107

awkward to bowl or even spin the ball again. It was thought that his first priority would be to have an operation on his shoulder. To undergo two major operations was something he couldn't contemplate. The risks were too great.

Signs of mortality gripped Warne as he brooded over what he should do. The pain and the most profound doubt a sportsman can ever have – that he may never play again – made him uncharacteristically irritable and tetchy with those around him. Just when he had reached his peak, his future looked bleak. And because he was now public property, his concerns became the public's concerns and he grew annoyed that everywhere he went people kept on asking him about it. Finally he had an operation on his finger. He also worked hard on bringing down his weight and underwent intense physiotherapy on his finger, but his worst fears were realised. His recovery was, for such an impatient man, very slow and he spoke publicly of his fears that he may never bowl again. It seemed no further proof was needed when after a long lay-off he returned to playing district cricket for St Kilda. Average batsmen had no trouble slogging him around the field. One-day games for Victoria further illustrated just how badly he was bowling. Afraid to use his finger too much in spinning the ball, he tried to concentrate on just being accurate, but it seldom helped him take wickets. He was made captain of the Victorian team and in the first game his bowling was innocuous, but in the next game against South Australia his bowling regained some of the spin and control of before and he was chosen for the First Test against the

West Indies in the 1996–97 season.

Warne's skills were noticeable in the First Test. He wasn't spinning the ball as far as he used to, but his nagging accuracy and subtle changes of pace were compensation for what he had lost. However, in the Second Test he bowled one of the most extraordinary deliveries of his career, revealing that his comeback was progressing better than he or his public had hoped. The West Indies had been set a large target of 340 runs and were in trouble early, having lost 3 for 35. But on the last morning the West Indies, taking the challenge given to them by Mark Taylor, who left the outfield vacant, attacked the bowling, including Warne. It was an exhilarating counter-attack of over a run a minute and the two batsmen, led by the left-hander Shivnarine Chanderpaul, who had scored 71, looked so at ease that there was a definite possibility they could win against Australia's flaccid and tired bowlers. Warne was given the last over before lunch.

Throughout his career Warne has managed to take wickets at crucial times and has an astounding ability to take them at the beginning or end of sessions, when batsmen are trying either to settle into a pattern of concentration or to maintain it as an interval break or the end of play beckons. The batsman's expectation that the mentally enervating battle with Warne is about to begin or is nearly over is when the leg spinner frequently gains a wicket. I was reminded of how frequently this happens when I arrived a few minutes late to the January, 2002 Third Test against South Africa only to discover that in his first over at the beginning of play Warne had already taken the important wicket of Jacques Kallis. Similarly in the First Test of the same series I was about to hit the remote control button and turn off the television as Warne prepared to bowl the last ball of the day, when Kirsten, the solid opening batsman, tapped an easy catch to a close infielder.

All this reminded me of the 1995 Pakistani tour of Australia. Warne, annoyed by Basit Ali's time-wasting behaviour in the Third Test in Sydney, decided to hold up play himself, before bowling the last ball of the day. Healy joined him in mid-pitch, supposedly to discuss tactics when really they were discussing where to have dinner that night. The sight of the two Australians apparently discussing ways of getting him out made Basit Ali uneasy. Instead of getting the last ball over and done with and dawdling off to the pavilion not out, he had to face what could be a new ploy against him. Warne bowled a ball that landed outside leg stump and Basit Ali, seemingly paralysed by the dread of what the ball might do, and determined not to play a stroke that could dismiss him, made a feeble gesture of placing a pad in the area where he hoped the ball might land, but once it hit the pitch the ball suddenly turned alarmingly, bouncing low, and darted between his pads to hit the stumps. Quite simply, Warne had preyed on Basit Ali's desire to get off the field and relax, and had undermined his concentration.

Almost exactly a year after dismissing Basit Ali and just two balls before lunch Warne came around the wicket to bowl to the seemingly impregnable Chanderpaul, who at this point in the match was confirmation that Warne found it more difficult to bowl to left-handers. Warne let go of the ball, with the confidence of someone who knew his spinning finger could now give the ball a huge twist of the wrist, and it went so far to the right of the West Indian batsman that on landing, had it gone straight on, it would have been called a wide. But the ball landed in the foot marks left by the fast bowlers and then abruptly jumped sideways, turning almost a metre. Chanderpaul, having momentarily believed it would be impossible for a ball to spin so far, suddenly found himself trying to fend off a delivery that Warne said was the furthest he had ever turned a ball. A moment after it hit the stumps, Chanderpaul glanced down at them and automatically turned around in the direction of the pavilion like a well-trained soldier programmed to do so and marched off. An excited Warne knew he had pulled off something spectacular and crouched down, pumping his fists in the air, yelling to himself. You could see in the exultant expressions of his team-mates, especially his captain, that Warne's wicket had ended any chance the West Indians had of winning the match. If a confident Chanderpaul could be beaten by such a ball, then the rest of the batsmen would be confused and beaten by doubt. And the delivery had a greater resonance, for it announced that Warne's comeback had been successful. The prodigious turn reminded batsmen everywhere that the Australian leg spinner was still more than capable of bowling unplayable deliveries.

Australia won the series and played the dead rubber in Perth on a pitch that was so cracked that Curtly

Ambrose's bat stuck in it in attempting to ground his bat after taking a run. It was Ambrose's last match in Australia. Tall as a basketballer, with a permanent sullen expression, he can be considered one of the greatest fast bowlers of all time, but unfortunately he lacked grace under pressure. His captain, Brian Lara, whose career has been bedevilled by a volatile mixture of batting genius and monstrous ego, became involved in a slanging match with the Australians over their sledging of the young batsman Robert Samuels, and Ambrose, buoyed up by his captain's indignation, decided that he would deliberately hurt the Australian player he despised the most. In a vicious and unprovoked assault on Warne, Ambrose deliberately no-balled by overstepping the crease – sometimes by up to half a metre – in order to make sure his bouncers would hit and hurt the spinner. In his last over, which took over twelve minutes and is regarded as one of the longest in Test cricket, Ambrose bowled fifteen balls, nine of which were deliberate no-balls. Ambrose's bouncers, delivered at such close range, were not only brutal and aimed at the head and body but were unpredictable, in that they might hit one of the many cracks, which meant the batsman had no way of telling whether a bouncer would pass harmlessly over his head or savagely deviate and thump into him. It was a spectacle more suitable to a mindless thug in crime-ridden Georgetown than a Test match. Up until then I had never seen such spiteful and savage behaviour on a cricket field. It seemed that Ambrose had waited several years to attack the man who had made West Indian batsmen look foolish with his sissy's knack of spinning the ball, and in revenge he delivered each ball with the cruel zeal of a streetfighter who wanted to maim. Despite Ambrose's deliberate need to inflict injury, Warne and Bichel made the largest stand of the Australian innings (55 runs) and in so doing Warne proved himself braver than the intimidating poltroon Ambrose.

It was also an illustration of Warne's batting ability, an ability that has always been apparent but which can be frustratingly inconsistent. When he was captain, Steve Waugh made constant digs at his spinner's average results with the bat, given his potential ability. By the time Warne finished the 2002 Test series in South Africa he had taken over four hundred wickets and scored 2000 runs but was yet to make a century. He has the dubious distinction of being third on the all-time list of runs without a century. He came tantalisingly close several times, a couple of times scoring 80s and in 2001 against New Zealand he came as close as you can when he scored 99 before impatiently having a swing at a ball that resulted in an outfield catch. Early in his career he made few runs, content to make sure that his spinning fingers, a natural target of fast bowlers, were not injured. It was later that he realised he was a better batsman than his batting average – which was in the middle teens – suggested and he began to try to settle in, but many a time his rambunctious impulses had him hitting more catches to the outfield than spectacular and crowd-pleasing sixes over the fence. Always a nervous starter, he has hung around to become involved in important partnerships and on several occasions helped Australia either draw a match (a memorable partnership with Ian

Healy in the 1995 Test against England, where they saved Australia with an unbroken stand on the final afternoon) or win one. In a tight finish in Cape Town in 2002, a nervous Warne joined Ponting as they tried to score the winning runs after chasing the substantial target of 334. His natural propensity to attack meant his first scoring shot was a slash for four that went perilously close to a slips fieldsman. This was followed quickly by a couple of hard-hit fours that broke the South Africans' spirit just when they sensed victory. In one-day games he was occasionally used as 'a pinch hitter', coming in to score quick runs when the scoring has bogged down, but he was never consistent enough. Since then Warne has been content to come in down the order and entertain the crowd by attempting to hit each ball over the fence, just as he would have when a teenager.

In 1997–98 he played Test series against South Africa, England and New Zealand. But since his finger operation, although his bowling had been consistently good he seemed incapable of reproducing his former match-winning efforts. In fact for almost two years he did not take five wickets in an innings. But in January, 1998, in the Second Test against South Africa in Sydney, he produced a remarkable spell of bowling, the last wicket of which, in an act that seemed pure showmanship, he produced his three-hundredth wicket. Warne had taken five wickets in the first innings, but it was on the fourth day, as the South Africans chased 134 to make Australia bat again, that he displayed his unique gift. In sultry conditions that promised, and eventually delivered, late rain, Warne mesmerised his opponents in a way similar

to placing a chook's head on the ground and drawing a
line away from its beak, causing it to fall in a trance.
Every delivery had the hypnotic effect of that line
drawn in the dirt, and the batsmen only woke from
their trance on hearing the stumps being hit or seeing
the umpire's finger raised. There is no better way to
illustrate Warne's increasingly shrewd analysis of his
opponents' strength than by studying his dismissal of the
grim-faced, Satan-fearing Hansie Cronje. Warne had
previously dismissed the South African captain by flight-
ing a ball down towards his leg stump. As it hit the pitch
and curled towards middle stump, Cronje played the ball
to the leg against the spin, tapping a catch to a close-in
fielder. Having stored the memory of that dismissal
away, Warne remembered it and bowled a very similar
ball again, and again Cronje did exactly the same thing,
this time getting in a tangle with pad and bat and sending a catch straight into the hands of the close-in fielder
on the leg side. Warne's next wicket, that of Hershelle
Gibbs, soon afterwards was almost a duplication of the
Cronje dismissal. Then he out-thought the tall, eagle-
eyed but stiff-legged McMillan with a ball that did not
turn. Watching the ball head directly towards leg stump,
McMillan shifted his weight ever so slightly towards the
off in order to play for the expected spin, but the ball
went straight on and hit the leg stump. It was a cagey
and subtle piece of bowling. The all-rounder Shaun
Pollock was out next when he carefully watched a
delivery drift towards leg stump. Realising that Warne
had imparted tremendous spin on the ball, Pollock leant
forward playing for the spin. He did everything right,

except that the ball deviated even more than he expected. It missed the middle of his bat, clipped the outside edge and was expertly caught at first slip by Mark Taylor, whose safe hands resulted in many a wicket to his leg spinner. The wicket-keeper came in as the incredulous Pollock slowly left the field, holding his breath until he expelled the foul air of disappointment in one long exasperated sigh. Dave Richardson did not last long either. He pushed forward to a full-length, harshly spinning ball. Caught between the temptation of wanting to thrash it or resigning himself to a defensive shot, he found himself bouncing on the mental trampoline of indecision and meekly hit the ball back to Warne for a simple caught-and-bowled. By this stage Warne had taken five wickets for 13 runs. From the non-striker's end, Jacques Kallis had watched his team-mates fumble and torment themselves while he scored a patient 45. After a rain break, Warne, having now reached 299 wickets, bowled a cunning trio of standard leg breaks, which Kallis duly played for. Thinking the fourth would be similar he studiously leaned forward but Warne had decided to bowl one that didn't turn. It was a top spinner that kept going straight on with the direction of his arm and found its way between the full face of the bat and Kallis's forward-leaning left pad. The sound of the ball hitting the stumps devastated Kallis, who thought it was impossible to penetrate what he imagined was the perfect defence. On seeing the ball hit the stumps to claim his three-hundredth wicket Warne uttered a loud guttural cry of joy, raising his arms and twisting his hands like batons. All doubts about his injury and recovery were gone in an exuberant celebration that was a mixture of relief, joy and amazement at his own skill.

Watching him bowl that day it seemed his skill was akin to music. The rhythm of his quick four-step walk in, the downswing beat of his arm as he let go of the ball, the *adagio* speed of his delivery and the surface melody of the ball's lovely arc seemed to be played in an inoffensive and predictable major key. But lurking in the subterranean depths was a minor key counter-theme that constantly threatened to undermine the pleasant harmony with a disturbing, sinister sound. It was one of the most superlative pieces of bowling you could ever wish to see and the crowd rose to applaud Warne's genius. You could see in their expressions not only pleasure at seeing him get his 300th wicket but also a real sense of delectation in having witnessed Warne elevating the craft and skill of leg spin bowling to a realm of achievement closer to aesthetic perfection than to a mundane physical activity. An elated Warne was determined to downplay any suggestion of arrogance and merely acknowledged the fact that when he first started he had little idea of what he was doing, but at this stage of his career: 'I think I know how to get [them] out now.' And with the 300 wickets came the realisation of having made real the daydreams of every cricket-loving boy: 'As a kid I was like any other youngster. I wanted to be Dennis Lillee, or Rod Marsh, or Ian Chappell. When I played backyard cricket with my brother, we had Rod Marsh behind the stumps, and we'd charge up and imitate Dennis Lillee or be Ian Chappell with the collar up, playing with your protector and all that sort of stuff. To be up in that company is an honour.'

But just when he was at the apex of what one may call the second act of his career, he found himself suddenly in the Slough of Despond, caused by a combination of injury, his nemesis, the Indian batsman Sachin Tendulkar, and the revelation of past indiscretions.

The Indians never seemed to hold Warne in great awe, but they knew they shouldn't be complacent. They had seen him bowl during the 1996 World Cup games in India. As Mike Marquesee wrote in *War Minus the Shooting*, his book about the 1996 World Cup, the Indian crowd were fascinated by Warne: 'It is a common belief that the Indians know how to play spin. The English and the West Indians might be befuddled by the likes of Warne, but surely not one of their own. So there is a desire to see Indian batsmen prove that Warne is nothing special. But there is also a fascination with the man, combining admiration for his amazing prestidigitation with a cricket ball, and bemusement at his personality – by turns buoyant, matey, whining and aggressive.'

They had also been following his progress closely through the immediacy of cable television, something that Australians underestimated. The Indian obsession with cricket even extends to a weekly television program about Australian interstate cricket. One who was determined to nullify Warne's potency was Sachin Tendulkar, whose batting technique, delicate footwork and greed for runs reminded Donald Bradman of himself. Like other bantam-sized batsmen, Border, Gavaskar and Bradman, he had an uncanny ability to avoid a bouncer.

(Although one time he was given out when, after duck-
ing so low the ball hit him on the helmet below the
level of the bails, he was given out leg before.)

Tendulkar studied Warne's bowling and meticulously
prepared for the Australian's first Test tour of India in
early 1998. During his long and intense practice sessions
he had deep scuff marks made outside his leg stump and
had leg spin bowlers bowl around the wicket at them,
aiming at the rough patch, knowing it would be Warne's
favourite tactic. Gradually Tendulkar refined his technique so that he was no longer vulnerable and upped
the ante by deciding to use his growing confidence not
to defend but to attack the Australian spinner. The Indians knew that Warne's shoulder was giving him such
trouble that he had pulled out of a short tour to New
Zealand in the hope of resting it before the Indian Tests.
Their plan was simple. Because the brilliant pace man
Glenn McGrath wasn't touring, the Australians would
have to depend on Warne to a much greater extent than
was normal, and if the Indians could hit him out of
the attack they would be a long way towards winning
the series. In order to undermine Warne's confidence,
Tendulkar decided to play against him in a warm-
up match in Bombay, something that important batsmen
occasionally shun so as to avoid being dismissed cheaply
and therefore giving the opponent a significant psychological victory. Tendulkar's assault on Warne was ruthless.
In keeping with his usual policy of never giving away
the full arsenal of his variations in lead-up games, Warne
saw his standard leg breaks being smacked all over the
ground as the Indian batsman made a double-century.

But in the first innings of the First Test in Chennai it appeared that Warne had outfoxed Tendulkar. The Indian had scored four and then, much to the silent horror of the spectators who were expecting their hero to pummel Warne into submission, the leg spinner made a ball drift and spin past Tendulkar, touching the edge of his bat, and Taylor took the catch at slip. But it proved to be the only time Warne ever looked like dominating the Indian batsmen, especially Tendulkar, who in the second innings thrashed him and the other Australian bowlers and made 155 not out. In the Second Test Warne was again remorselessly hammered by Tendulkar and his fellow batsmen who had gained much confidence from Tendulkar's savage offensive on the Australian. Warne's figures of no wicket for 147 runs were among the worst of his career. Tendulkar's planning had worked perfectly. In destroying Warne he had demoralised the whole Australian team and made the Australians realise just how much they relied on their spinner. After losing the first two Tests, it was obvious that without Warne performing at his best against such good players of spin, Australia's attack was inadequate and ineffectual.

Warne's damaged shoulder was growing worse and his confidence was the lowest it had been since his inauspicious entry into Test cricket. *The Australian's* cricket writer Mike Coward, who it must be said is a partisan and sometimes wearying proselytiser of Indian and Pakistan cricket and culture, summed up the tour: 'Australia are world champions in Test cricket except in one regard – they cannot win on the subcontinent – and if they cannot win here, what sort of champions are they really?'

Back in Australia the specialists who examined Warne thought that if he had played just a few more games his shoulder would have been beyond repair. As it was, the damage was considerable. He had tears of the cuff tendon and labrum (a ring of cartilage that lines the edge of the shoulder socket) and extensive scarring. His rehabilitation was fraught with uncertainties. Would the operation work and just how long would recovery take? Even after his shoulder was repaired, would he be able to bowl as well as he had formerly? Warne missed the Commonwealth Games tournament in Malaya and Australia's successful tour of Pakistan. The English tour of Australia approached and he was determined to play in it, and worked hard at his rehabilitation despite additional surgery.

Six months later he played a one-day game and captained Victoria in a Sheffield game. His bowling was barely adequate and his talent seemed to be in irreversible decline. He didn't think that things could get much worse. But they did. A secret that had remained hidden for four years now seeped out into the public domain through a dogged newspaper reporter. Warne was again back in the headlines and his career was now at stake.

8: It Doesn't Rain but it Pours

Over several nights in 1994, in a casino in the Sri Lanka capital of Colombo, an Indian man had patiently watched two Australian cricketers. One was Mark Waugh and the other Shane Warne. Both were well-known gamblers. Waugh's comment that 'the form guide is my favourite reading matter' summed up his fanatical interest in horseracing. He was known to have pretended an injury during one cricket match in order to get off the field and listen to an important race. He is among a number of habitual gamblers in Australian cricket, including the charismatic all-rounder Keith Miller and wicket-keeper Wally Grout, the latter's gambling so dominating his life that it could be best classed as not so much a pastime as an addiction.

Over the years, whenever he has had problems with his bowling Warne has sought out Terry Jenner for advice. Like Grout, Jenner was addicted to gambling but kept it secret from his fellow players during his Test career. 'Many people, even those close to me like Ian Chappell,' he has written, 'never knew I had a gambling problem. There was hardly any gambling at all among the Australian teams I played with. Until Ken Eastwood was picked for a Test at the end of the 1970–71 summer I'd never seen another Test cricketer with a form guide in his back pocket. In the West Indies in 1973 only Ross Edwards was interested in roulette. Dougie Walters was into cards. Some cricketers would go to the trots and while most of the boys would have just one or two bets, I'd have to bet on every race.' The tenacious grip of his addiction is well illustrated in an anecdote about going to an illegal casino in Darlinghurst one night: 'I took $40 with me and soon lost it. Another Australian cricketer also lost his money playing roulette. Next minute he was cashing in his Test match payment cheque. I couldn't believe it. In my wildest times I wouldn't have done that. It was sacrilege. He bought $230 worth of chips, backed evens and it came up. He collected the money and left. I stayed, watched a little more and cashed my cheque too. I lost the lot.' The outcome of Jenner's obsession was predictable. Much money lost, a need to pay back the bookies and the answer to the shortfall – embezzlement; the result, prison.

His advice to the young man about cricket was always excellent, yet one had to wonder if the two of them ever talked about Warne's fondness for gambling, especially roulette and blackjack, given its potential danger as an addiction? Border sees Warne's interest in gambling as part of his competitive nature: 'For Shane Warne, life is a competition. Go round the golf course with him and he can't help it, he has to have a few side bets. Go to the casino with him and he has to try his luck ... Get him on the cricket field, of course, and he'll back himself to do anything.' Warne bets considerable amounts of money on roulette, frequently playing 23 red, the number he wore as a St Kilda footballer. Given his failure at that level there is an element of perversity in believing in the magical properties of the number.

In September, 1994 Australia was playing in one of the increasingly forgettable one-day tournaments in Sri Lanka before going on to Pakistan for a Test series. The nearest casino was not far from the team hotel and Waugh and Warne were regulars. The Indian who had taken a covert interest in the two Australians approached Waugh and engaged him in a conversation. At the time Warne paid little heed to what his teammate was doing because he was in the process of playing roulette. After losing about US$5000, Warne joined Waugh, who introduced him to the Indian, who impressed the two Australians as a wealthy cricket fan by the name of John. No-one knows to this day if this was a pseudonym or not, and physical descriptions are vague, lost in the haze of generalities that occurs when Australians try to identify the characteristics of individual Indians. He also mentioned that he liked to bet on cricket. Retrospectively this was a subtle distinction for Warne. Someone who bets on cricket is 'quite different from being a bookmaker'. Quite so. John spent the next thirty minutes flattering Warne, calling him his favourite player, then the pair shook hands and the Australians

returned to their hotel. The next day, after John called
Warne and invited him to his room, they realised that
the Indian was also staying at their hotel – coinciden-
tally. Warne went to John's room where the Indian
praised him even more than the previous night, but, as
the Australian spinner has remarked, 'most cricketers
become used to [flattery] on the subcontinent'.

What happened next rattled the leg spinner. John
gave him a plump envelope filled with money. When
Warne asked what the money was for, the unctuous,
pleasant Indian said it was a token of appreciation for
the wonderful cricket Warne had played and a compensation for the money he had lost at the roulette table the
previous night. Warne thanked him for his kindness but
refused to take it, saying he had plenty of his own
money, but the Indian was insistent, telling him that he
was very wealthy and would be offended if he didn't.
Believing it was merely a gift, Warne took the money
and with an alacrity common to dogged gamblers lost
all of it at the casino that same night. Warne was to discover that Waugh had also been given money by the
magnanimous 'John'. No doubt the two of them had a
bit of a laugh about those crazy, generous Indians, and
did not give more thought to why a man would be so
liberal with his money.

Both Australians had been warned by their coach,
Bob Simpson, to be on guard against people offering
gifts. 'I have no reason whatsoever to doubt his word,'
Warne writes in his autobiography, 'but it certainly
didn't register with me.' His excuse was that team meet-
ings have a tendency to drag on for hours and such

warnings are unheard by a brain that is caught up in the genial static of daydreaming. Warne also excuses himself by dint of the fact that the incident happened way back in 1994 when 'none of us imagined how aspects of the game might be corrupt ... The idea that bookmakers might be trying to buy up cricketers could have come from a work of fiction. We also knew there were some generous people in the subcontinent who were fanatical about the game. There were stories about players being given cars and gold nuggets simply as a mark of appreciation.'

Although Warne was to meet John only the two times in Colombo the Indian proved to be an indefatigable schmoozer, ringing him wherever he might be, wishing him Happy Christmas and Happy Birthday and inquiring, almost as an afterthought, or so it seemed to the Australian, about the weather in whatever part of the world Warne happened to be in and whether the wicket on which the Australian was about to play would suit spin. Warne has always said that he was never under the impression he was giving information to a bookmaker. Yet Warne was aware of a tradeoff: the Indian had given him a financial gift and in return Warne was giving him his time and information about the match he was to play. It seems strange that the Indian was always able to call Warne, when he is known to be notoriously unreliable in answering his phone or returning messages. His defence was straightforward: 'Technically, I did give information for money, but it was not in the way it has been portrayed.' As far as he is concerned, he gave the media more important information for free than he

ever gave the generous Indian. Amidst this retrospective
bluster there is the familiar Warne equivocation in ratio-
nalising his behaviour by hinting that it was not all his
doing: 'I just assumed he was a mate of Mark's who was
having a bet on cricket.'

Later, following a script written for them, both
Waugh and Warne were to say publicly that their actions
were 'naive and stupid', and perhaps this is true, given
that a few weeks later Salim Malik offered Warne money
to throw the First Test against Pakistan. Only now is
Warne aware that Malik, whose match-fixing propensi-
ties were to result in his expulsion from the game six
years later, must have had connections with John and the
Indian must have informed the Pakistani that the Australian spinner had a weakness for gambling and had
accepted money in return for information, admittedly
of limited value. It didn't occur to Warne that there must
have been a reason why he had been targeted twice and
offered money both times.

Warne becomes rather fuzzy with specific dates
about who he told and when, and just when they in
turn told the Australian authorities about Malik's
bribery offer at the Pearl Continental hotel three weeks
after the casino meeting with John. He writes in *Shane
Warne, My Autobiography* that after Malik had made the
offer he and May told captain Mark Taylor – who was
captaining the side for the first time – about the
approach and that 'he in turn passed the information to
Bobby Simpson, our coach and Col Egar, our manager,
who reported it to John Reid, the match referee'. But it
seems it wasn't as simple and straightforward as that.

Taylor was an inspiring leader, but he was criticised by some for not taking greater responsibility for events off the field, and seemed to be saying in his earliest comments about the affair that he immediately told Simpson and Egar about the bribery offer. But he contradicted himself later when he wrote that he kept the matter to himself. The kindest excuse is that it was his first Test as captain and he didn't want to be taxed by problems unrelated to winning the match, and didn't realise the true significance of what had occurred. May himself says he didn't say anything about the matter until some weeks later, on October 22 at Rawalpindi before a one-day game against Pakistan. On that occasion Malik approached Waugh and offered him, his brother Steven, Warne and May $US50,000 to 'put in a stinker'. Waugh apparently rejected the offer but the persistent Malik made another an hour or so later. The next day Australia lost the game (Mark Waugh top scoring with 121 not out) and, according to May in an unpublished interview with the magazine *Inside Sport*, when the defeated Australians returned to the pavilion, '[Mark] walked in the rooms – we hadn't told anybody about these bribes and that sort of stuff, we thought it was just … hush. Like, "Christ, did this really happen?" And Mark Waugh said [as a joke], "Ah, would've been better off taking the bribes, guys." And the manager [Col Egar] and coach [Simpson] were there – "What? What are you talking about?" And so that's where it all sort of came from.'

There the matter seemed to rest and Warne had an excellent series against England and then in February, 1995 went on a short tour of New Zealand for another

series of one-day games. It was there that Warne
received another phone call – the telephone has played
a pivotal role at crucial points in his life. This time it was
Ian McDonald, the team manager, who had seen Warne
progress from a chubby failure to a slimmed down success, who was inviting the spinner to his room. He asked
the apprehensive Warne if he knew about players taking
money for providing weather and pitch reports. Warne
said no. His excuse is as subtle and slick as anything
by Bill Clinton during the Monica Lewinsky affair. 'I
was not trying to deceive McDonald by being clever,
because when John gave me five thousand dollars he
wanted nothing in return. Besides which, what we
talked about was just general chat.' Warne told McDonald that the only money he had received was from the
occasional sportsmen's dinner and 'a gift from a guy
who was a friend of Mark Waugh'. Then having palmed
off any responsibility, which is Warne's way, he had to
listen to McDonald ask him if the man named John was
in any way the same Indian with whom Mark Waugh
had a business arrangement to provide information
about the weather and the state of the pitches. Warne
remembers 'getting that sinking feeling'. He told the
team manager the whole story; contradicting his previously hazy denial, he admitted that 'Yes, I did speak to
["John"] about pitches and weather.' What puzzled
Warne as he trooped back to his room was 'how he got
wind there might be a problem in the first place'. It has
always been exasperating to Warne that no matter how
deeply a secret has been hidden, the damn truth seems
to ooze its way up to the surface.

McDonald told the Australian Cricket Board about his meeting with Warne and when the spinner was briefly back in Australia before flying off to the West Indies, he and Waugh were interviewed by the ACB. The decision on their cricketing future was unresolved when the duo left Sydney for the West Indies and a nervous Warne wondered whether, when he and Waugh arrived in the Caribbean, they were going to be sent back to Australia immediately. At a stopover in London both men were told they would be fined, Warne $8000 and Waugh $10,000. The ACB also decided to keep the decision secret from the public. For Warne this was good news because 'I felt I'd done nothing wrong. We all make mistakes'. The ACB made sure their own tracks were covered by not entering the deal in the official minutes.

The Australian Cricket Board's decision was to have many repercussions. Its actions seem to have been determined by the practical consideration of winning the series against the West Indies and bringing back the Frank Worrell Trophy. Warne's fear that he might be pulled from the tour was groundless, for the simple reason that he was crucial to beating the team that had walloped Australia over the years. Warne had been persisted with and groomed for precisely this occasion. No way was the ACB, which had invested so much time in him, especially earlier in his career, going to hobble Australia's attempt to wrench back the prize. A controversy over giving cricket information for money would only destabilise the team. It was hard enough to win against the West Indies in Australia let alone on their home soil, scattered as it may be across many islands.

Warne arrived with the familiar media fanfare that was to greet him in every country where he was to play. As West Indian commentator Tony Cozier said, 'No spin bowler has ever arrived in the Caribbean with greater advance than the bouncy, blond leg spinner.' Peeved at the attention Warne was getting and deciding on a deliberate policy of assaulting his bowling in order to hit him out of the attack, the West Indian batsmen started on the Australian during the First Test, and after his first few overs Warne's poor figures indicated just how successful they had been. But just when it seemed as though the spinner was wilting under the pressure, he took five wickets in a match Australia won. By the time the final Test came around the series score was one all. Australia won the fourth and deciding game with Warne taking six wickets, including the valuable one of Brian Lara. He hadn't dominated the series but he had played a decisive role in the victory and, as such, justified the ACB's decision to fine Waugh and he in-house. It was the first time since 1973 that the West Indian team had been beaten at home. After the defeat, Richie Richardson, their captain, was ungracious as usual, calling the Australians the worst team he had ever played against, which said a lot for the quality of his own players.

News and gossip about matches being fixed began to circulate through the cricket world as more people heard about Malik's clumsy attempt to bribe the Australian players. The first reaction, especially from the authorities, was one of bumbling incomprehension. After all, there had been almost a century of cricket untarnished by any suggestion of match-fixing and illegal betting. Cricket had given the British Empire phrases such as 'A gentlemen's game', 'Play by the rules', 'It's not cricket' and 'Play with a straight bat'. But these expressions of proper behaviour were not a product of the early history of the game, which was marred by betting scandals and match-fixing in much of the Victorian era. An early tour by the English team to Australia indicated just how much the culture of betting had seeped into the colony's cricket when in February, 1879 English captain Lord Harris was attacked with a stick and a team-mate punched by an angry mob during a riot at the Sydney Cricket Ground when an Australian was given run out. Punters were incensed at the decision and detected in the feeble cricket of the English during the earlier part of the tour a deliberate scheme to get their team better odds. Play was abandoned for the day as the furious gamblers invaded the field.

Gradually the game was cleaned up, so successfully in the twentieth century that cricket became a byword for ethical behaviour and sportsmanship. Even now, cricket is one of the few sports where the opposition will applaud an opponent's skilfully realised score or gallant rearguard action during the actual game itself. What cricket followers and authorities underestimated were two potent factors surrounding the game on the sub-continent – betting and poverty. The Indian betting industry is huge. Betting on horses is legal but the taxes on winnings are considerable, so for punter and bookie alike it is much more attractive to engage in illegal betting. Illegal betting on one-day games flourishes to such an extent that it is reliably reported by the *Times of India* that approximately $US6–9 billion is bet on matches played by India alone in a year. The bets are not only on the outcome of a match, but other eventualities such as who will make the highest score, who will make a duck and who will hit the most fours or sixes. The permutations are almost limitless, and radio listeners and television viewers watch a game knowing that practically every score or wicket taken has a betting plunge attached to it.

The amount of money involved is so vast that it is not surprising that players are approached to help fix a game or that single players are enticed to score less than expected. Added to this is something that cricketers from wealthy countries fail to appreciate. For some sub-continental players, cricket is a way out of poverty or a way to make certain of financial security once you are retired, given that in these countries the welfare state is all but non-existent. A young player from Sri Lanka, Pakistan or India, suddenly finding himself in a plush hotel or luxury restaurant for the first time and having tasted the delights of this lifestyle, wants it to continue. The large extended families who depend on their famous son, nephew or cousin make their financial demands too, believing that the shared abundance from their generous relative will continue as long as they desire it; this adds more pressure on the player to earn more money. Into the mix of a lack of money and illegal gambling comes the most potent ingredient – the enormous number of one-day games being played. There may be the occasional international contest that has some sort of purpose because it entails national pride but the majority of one-day games are merely money-making events for cricket authorities and there is the natural reaction of many cricketers to not try as hard as one would in a Test match and hope that the relentless blur of constant one-day games slackens, but it never does, and there are many games which seem totally pointless to both teams, no matter who wins or loses. So if that is the case, then why not fix them? For the needy or the greedy the temptation to throw a match or bat against form in order to make much more than the match fee is patent and insidious.

As rumours grew about Salim Malik's overtures to Warne and Waugh, suspicions began to materialise about certain matches where the results had gone contrary to form and expectations. These invariably involved the Pakistani team, although India was not exempt.

The malodorous ooze of corruption was percolating up into the open everywhere. In February, 1995, Phil Wilkins, reporting for the *Sydney Morning Herald*, wrote that a Pakistani player had unsuccessfully tried to bribe Warne, May and Waugh the previous year. Soon identified as the Pakistani player, an outraged Malik denied the accusation and, pleading his innocence, told the media he was going to take legal action. But it was all bluster. There were too many people who knew of Malik's role in match-fixing. The Pakistani authorities were, of course, extremely interested in Warne, Waugh and May's allegations of Malik's several offers. The wary trinity made sworn but timid statements and the Australian Cricket Board refused to allow them to appear before the inquiry in Pakistan. The Board's excuse was that it was 'an internal Pakistan matter' and, of course, there were veiled hints that the trio could be in physical danger if they went to Pakistan. The usual stereotypes of lawless, unscrupulous and untrustworthy Pakistanis were trotted out. But the reality is much more murky than what was aired in public.

The ACB had a problem. Well, two problems in fact – Warne and Waugh. There was no way that the Board could take the high moral ground. It had covered up the duo's misdemeanours and if the secret got out then the whole problem of illegal betting and bribery would, in the eyes of the cricket world, also incriminate the Australians. There was probably a sigh of relief from members of the ACB when, in October, 1994, Malik was exonerated by the judge heading the Pakistani inquiry. Fakhruddin G. Ebrahim called the Australians' allegations 'unbelievable'. A happy and unrepentant Malik chortled that the reason why Warne raised the allegations was because the spinner couldn't take his wicket once in the 1994 series.

The ACB may have been relieved that the Malik verdict meant its secret would remain undetected but Warne was incensed by Malik's remarks about him after being found not guilty. In November, 1995 Australia played Pakistan in the First Test in Brisbane. Warne not only wanted to prove he was a threat to the Pakistani batsmen, he wanted revenge on the man the Australians called 'The Cheat' and 'The Rat'. Warne thought he'd bowl bouncers at Malik when he came into bat. Sensibly, captain Mark Taylor told him to stick to bowling what he did best – leg spin. The previously imperturbable Malik, now in a foreign country and surrounded by fielders eerily silent as they gave him the cold shoulder treatment, lasted only several balls before delivering a soft catch to mid-off. The dismissal was a vindication for Warne. As far as he was concerned 'there is justice in the game'. If the Pakistanis thought Warne wasn't the potent bowler he had been they were abruptly reminded of his gift in the First Test where the Australian spinner took eleven wickets for the match, the best figures by an Australian against them.

Justice and vindication may be easier to achieve on the cricket field than in real life, and out on the field Warne could convince himself that the Malik and the match-fixing saga was over, but the corruption controversy was snowballing. In early 1996 Pakistani Intelligence bugged the telephones of several Test cricketers. The evidence was clear that some players were still in touch with bookmakers. Other Pakistani cricketers came forward, accusing fellow players of having tried to bribe them. Even Pakistani umpire Javed Akhtar had to refute accusations that he had given several dubious l.b.w. decisions against South Africa in order to ensure England won a crucial Test. In September, 1998 the Pakistani Cricket Board announced that Malik, Wasim Akram and Ijaz Ahmed were guilty of match-fixing. The following month, Mark Waugh and Mark Taylor, now touring Pakistan, minus Warne who was still recovering from his shoulder operation, attended an in-camera hearing inquiring into match-fixing. Waugh, as skilfully as he used to evade the most lethal bouncer, avoided telling the inquiry of his own involvement with bookmakers but the tight skein of secrecy and evasion was unravelling.

Malcolm Conn, a reporter for *The Australian*, began to investigate rumours about several Australian players, including one in particular who might be involved in match-fixing. Gradually he pieced together a pattern of official concealment of Mark Waugh's involvement with shady bookmakers. It was at Ian Healy's nightclub in Brisbane at the beginning of the 1998 Ashes series that Conn ran into an informant who held the key piece of information. He was told that four years previously the ACB had secretly fined Waugh for trading information for money with illegal Indian bookmakers. At this stage Conn hadn't heard of Warne's participation in all of this, but when he told the ACB he was going to break the story about Waugh's dealings with Indian bookmakers it had no alternative than to tell him that Warne was also entangled in the mess.

Realising the news was about to break, the Board rushed to explain its position and excused its actions of not publicly reporting Warne and Waugh's involvement with bookmakers, saying that at the time it was an internal disciplinary matter. Warne and Waugh were quickly rounded up and instructed what to say at a press conference. 'During the course of the 1994 tour of Sri Lanka,' Warne said, reading out the statement, 'before we went to Pakistan, I was approached by a man who I later discovered to be a bookmaker from India. He gave me $5000 and in return he spoke to me on several occasions with pretty routine questions like what the pitch was like and what the weather conditions were. I never at any stage told him about team tactics or selection. As the captain of Victoria and a senior Australian cricketer I regularly provide much more detailed information to the media before any match I play. However, I realise I was very naive and stupid. I was fined $8000 by the ACB and paid the fine immediately. I've had no contact with the bookmaker since and I'm very disappointed and sorry for my actions.' After reading their statements both men refused to answer questions, but you could see in Warne's expression a barely containable sense of irritated bewilderment as to why there was all this fuss. He could understand the natural justice in taking Malik's wicket but the public outrage and calls for him to be sacked genuinely puzzled him. He seemed to be thinking it was all so simple out there on that green oval of grass and the strip of turf that had become his stage and his territory, but step through the picket gate off the field and suddenly it was another world, something primitive and primal compared to the rules and regulations of cricket. God, one moment you're called a Sultan, a Wizard, a Genius, and the next there is a frenzy of self-righteous indignation, abuse and ridicule when all you did was accept a gift from a damn Indian whose name you've forgotten. Everything makes sense on the cricket paddock but just take one step off it and people either want to sidle up to you and bask in your reflected glory or they want a bloody piece of you. And the worst are those fucking hyenas, jackals, piranhas, call them what you will, who write about you, who owe their livelihood to you.

At first, when the news broke, the ACB thought the controversy would be brief. It had no idea how shocked the public would be that two leading Australian players had been involved with illegal bookmakers and that the Board had tried to cover it up. The ACB just didn't understand that cricket lovers were appalled that their game had become tainted. Cricket was supposed to be above money and tampering. The game was a byword for fairness and honour. As the scandal spread the Board was pressured into holding an independent inquiry into what was becoming a frenzy of criticism, mud slinging and trial by innuendo. Even innocent players were shocked to find themselves under public and press speculation about their past performances on the cricket field.

The inquiry was thorough and in the final report scathing towards the Board and especially Warne and Waugh. In the report the ACB came across as arrogant and not a little stupid in its failure to 'conclude that there was no connection between "John's" payments and [Malik's] alleged attempted bribes'. As far as the greedy duo were concerned the inquiry criticised them for having 'failed lamentably to set the sort of example one might expect from senior players and role models for young cricketers'. The head of the inquiry also suggested that the proper response of the Board should have been to give the duo 'substantial suspensions' rather than fines.

But as the ACB had conspired to keep the bookie scandal quiet it could not punish Warne and Waugh without seeming hypocritical. Ignoring criticism, the Board made Warne and Waugh captain and vice-captain respectively of the one-day team. Journalists and the public were appalled. The bookmaking scandal undermined people's faith in the belief that, unlike the subcontinental cricketers, Australia's Test players were above greed, corruption and tawdry deals. 'Shame' and 'National Humiliation' were some of the newspaper headlines. Waugh was booed when he walked to the wicket to bat for Australia against England in the Adelaide Test. Normally unflappable and laconic, he bumbled his way to a low score, playing like a blind cricketer who lunges hopefully at where he thinks he heard the ball bounce. Warne was fired from his newspaper column. He missed the substantial money his column earned and still did not understand why he was being condemned. He tried to avoid the controversy by focusing all his endeavours on improving his shoulder and returning to the Test team, but he was struggling to take wickets for Victoria and, bowed down by the scandal, captained the State side in an uncharacteristically timid fashion.

It became apparent that Warne had been involved neither in match fixing nor giving important information for money to bookmakers. This became quite clear when Warne sued the *Herald Sun* newspaper for a front-page article titled 'Match Fix', which claimed that he had taken money for a match that was fixed. The long-running damages claim was finally settled in late April, 2002 when Warne won a page-three apology and an undisclosed payout.

An intrepid judicial investigation by Pakistan's Justice Qayyum in 2000 recommended a life ban for Salim Malik. Half a dozen other players were also cited as being part of a deliberate deception and were fined for associating with illegal bookmakers and withholding evidence. Malik protested his innocence but no-one believed him. It seemed that corruption was limited to the subcontinent (with the exception of Sri Lankan cricketers) but, in the same year as Justice Qayyum delivered his report, allegations of corruption were levelled at Alex Stewart, the English batsman and wicket-keeper (although who could believe that the English team could ever contrive a result, given that they found winning almost impossible?) and Hansie Cronje, the South African captain.

When Cronje was first accused of match-fixing it was impossible to believe that this grim man, who took defeat so badly against Australians that one time he smashed a stump through the door of an umpires' room, would have been involved in such tawdry behaviour. He was wealthy, he led a team that was one of the best in the world (though prey to their captain's siege mentality which stifled adventure, so they won through an unattractive game based on attrition) and so hated losing that it seemed inconceivable he would countenance the idea of sacrificing a win for money. But in April, 2000 he admitted his guilt and, in the contemporary vogue of not taking responsibility for one's actions but seeing himself as a hapless victim, he blamed Satan for his greed. (He avoided gaol but the gods or even Satan himself seemed to determine another fate for him when two years later, after missing a scheduled flight, he decided to return home in a cargo plane that crashed, killing the disgraced former captain and the two pilots.)

As Warne struggled to overcome people's perception of him as a greedy opportunist, his slow-mending shoulder meant his Sheffield Shield form was mediocre at best. He was desperately keen to return to Test cricket and eager to blunt the threat of the NSW leg spinner, Stuart MacGill, whose occasional appearances in the Test team were very successful. Although not fit to play Test cricket, Warne managed to convince the selection panel that he was ready for the Fifth Test against England in January, 1999. And for a brief time it seemed a good decision. The Sydney crowd, much more forgiving than the Adelaide spectators who had been so hostile to Mark Waugh, cheered Warne when he came on to bowl. Being the showman he is, he was immediately successful in his first over, claiming Mark Butcher's wicket with a leg break so tame that it didn't spin. It was a premature celebration of his return to Test cricket because he only gained one more wicket for the match, and had to watch helplessly as MacGill spun the ball superbly and took 12 wickets in the game. The experience of having to play second fiddle to another leg spinner, who was patently bowling better than he was, permanently scarred Warne. He could barely conceal his annoyance in the future when it was suggested that MacGill bowl in tandem with him. The knowledge that MacGill was also in the team to tour the West Indies irritated him and he was determined to prove that it was he and not the New South Welshman who was indispensable to the Australian team. The team was being captained for the first time by Steve Waugh, whose dislike of losing was such a natural part of his being that as a child he would go to the lengths of deliberately tripping up his twin, Mark, if it meant he would win a foot race.

Waugh's innate toughness was to be rigorously tested during the series against the West Indies because, after Australia won the First Test easily, Brian Lara almost single-handedly won the next two Test matches, the third one in a thrilling one-wicket victory that seemed to prove that Warne was a spent force. Unlike MacGill, Warne bowled lamely and without conviction in the series. He seemed unable to trust his wonky shoulder and, rather than pitching and spinning the ball to where he wanted it to go, seemed to be mentally willing it to go where his shoulder couldn't direct it. Against a left-hander like Lara his barely spinning deliveries were frequently not on the right spot and were mercilessly thrashed. Warne's inability to make an important break-through in the Third Test convinced Waugh that his vice-captain's position in the side was becoming increasingly unjustified. Warne took some convincing that he should be dropped. There was the usual bluster, the appeal to his past successes and the promise that his return to form was imminent, but it didn't work and he was left out of the team for the fourth and final Test. For Waugh and his co-selector Geoff Marsh it was one of the toughest decisions they had ever had to make. But it was the right one because the Australians levelled the series by winning the Fourth Test without him. Warne was shattered. The nearest comparison to what he felt was the time years before when he had been dropped from the St Kilda football team.

He felt a sharp sense of betrayal. It was bad enough to be hounded and criticised by the media, but to have his captain and coach humiliate him was awful. If he couldn't even depend on his team-mates then what was the damn use of playing anymore? He had given his heart and soul to the Australian Test team and what was his thanks? Two men who couldn't even look him in the eye when they gave him the news had decided he wasn't good enough to play Test cricket. Well, if that was the case then he might as well give the game away. His usual ebullient self was replaced by a surly, embittered silence and when he did speak it was to talk about retirement. 'I have to have a serious think about what I want to do in the future,' he said, hoping that people would come to his defence. But after all the controversies, the bookie scandal and the poor form, few did. Besides that, he was in the West Indies and a world away from his usual supporters. It was left to his wife, Simone, to massage his bruised ego by telling him he had nothing left to prove. No doubt she would be relieved if he did retire from the game because the fierce and unrelenting spotlight on her husband had been at considerable cost to their private life from the very day they had married.

9: 'My Life is a Soap Opera'

'My life has become a soap opera,' Warne said in 1999 after numerous controversies, scandals, setbacks and successes. And who could blame him for his sense of exasperation? He just didn't seem to be able to stay out of trouble. And for a man who has tried to maintain his privacy off the field, the attention his personal life has attracted continues to vex him. Even his wedding had involved controversy.

In 1992 Warne met a promotions model at a celebrity golf tournament. Blonde, attractive, with sanitised 'girl next door' looks, Simone Callahan had an eerie similarity to Warne when he was at his svelte best. They were blond, with similar foreheads, almond-shaped eyes, mouths and even chins. They could have been brother and sister. Having dated and travelled together they married on September 1, 1995. Warne tried to keep the event private. He rejected offers from women's magazines and television to cover the wedding. Even the

BBC offered a rumoured figure of $200,000 in order to do a 'fly on the wall' documentary about the wedding. The Beeb, intrigued by the Down Under suburban world of *Neighbours* and the gross materialism of the series *Sylvania Waters*, realised that the wedding would be perfect for English viewers. They could salivate over the mixture of money and celebrity and snigger over the opulent tastelessness of Australians. But by 1995 Warne was already wealthy and he didn't need the money or the attention. He rejected all offers from the media trying to grab exclusive rights and even went to the extent of hiring security guards for the wedding and reception at Como House, for years regarded as a prime example of Victorian architecture and proof of the wealth and supreme confidence in the future that the State once symbolised.

But a few weeks later *Woman's Day* published a two-page spread featuring photographs from the wedding. The Warnes were appalled. Apparently the photographs had been pilfered from or handed on from a Rabbit Photo shop where a guest had sent three rolls of film from the wedding to be developed, only to discover that seven prints were missing when the photographs were handed over. As far as the Warnes were concerned this was a gross invasion of their privacy. They could have sued *Woman's Day* but as it was part of the large stable of magazines owned by Kerry Packer, the media tycoon, who also employed him at Channel 9, a different strategy had to be utilised. The Warnes sued the photo outlet for $150,000, claiming that this was the amount they could have earned if they had decided to sell exclusive rights to the wedding. The case dragged on for some time until an out-of-court settlement was reached.

This was to be one of many examples of the invasion of his private life. From then on Warne was to be constantly reminded of what an equivocal accomplishment being a celebrity can be. The split between private and public life that a normal person takes for granted becomes a fusion of both worlds for a celebrity and everything he does becomes public property. Warne, who has supped with the contemporary devils – television and advertising – has frequently found it difficult to develop a dividing line between his celebrity and his private life. But as he was to learn, being a celebrity can be a disturbing interchange between the celebrity and his audience. Sooner or later – and in Warne's case, later – a celebrity realises that he is not an independent creation. His audience believes it has created him. So magazine and newspaper readers and television viewers demand the right to know everything about the person and find satisfaction and voyeuristic delight by insinuating themselves into the celebrity's private life. The celebrity's successes are theirs too, but the celebrity's public failures and mistakes are seen as a rightful correction to the egocentric behaviour and cockiness. A fascination with a celebrity also entails a degree of *schadenfreude*. The very people who are obsessed with celebrities want the person they venerate to make mistakes so that he can be brought down to their level. But they do offer an attractive exchange to the errant celebrity: they are the only ones who can offer forgiveness and redemption, but at a price. Celebrities will have to make public confessions about their private sins and misdemeanours, and in our world of rubbery moralism and lack of memory, once the celebrity is forgiven then all the sins are forgotten. It is a mutual and unspoken pact of codependence.

Warne would slowly learn this lesson, but in the early days of his fame he was still astonished at the public's obsession with him. Tour buses stopped outside his house, people brazenly peered through his curtains, and others openly stared at him if he were in the street. The attention unnerved Warne and his wife and they were forced to shift to a less-known location where they could indulge in creating a suburban world that reflected their *nouveau riche* tastes, like the white carpets and white couches that could easily have belonged to the family in *Sylvania Waters*.

Warne is the most famous cricketer since Sir Donald Bradman, but unlike the great batsman, the leg spinner is gregarious and not as shrewd. Bradman had a canny knowledge of the stock market and a craving to withdraw from the monotonously intense media interest in him. And of course Bradman did not play cricket in the late twentieth century. He did not have to face the increasingly large corps of cricket writers, many of whom no longer report the match in detail (television does that with an unrivalled immediacy) but proffer analysis, write exhaustive player profiles and report on what is happening off the field. In Bradman's era there were not the tabloid 'stings' and the grubby techniques of offering money to women for sordid details of extramarital flings. Instead of one movie camera lens positioned so far from the action that the brief newsreel coverage of matches was akin to watching cricket through the wrong end of a telescope, television has its many probing cameras which report and replay everything of consequence that happens on the field, including swearing, picking of noses and abrasive exchanges. And finally there wasn't the shamelessness of the present era. Two or three decades ago a mere indirect mention in the press that a woman may have had an affair with a married man would have stained her reputation forever. These days some women are quite happy – for a large fee – to report on having slept with a famous sportsman or movie star.

Test cricket is interesting for its patient relationship with time. A match can last five days – in one infamous occasion a Test match went ten days without a result – and, given that a tour may have five Tests and many three- or four-day games, the length of the tours is almost unique for a sport. Before airplanes a tour of Australia by the English or vice versa could take up to six months. It's a long time to be away from home. Even now the tours are long and tiresome. As Frances Edmonds writes in *Another Bloody Tour*: 'It is pointless to pretend that three- and four-month tours are not going to involve a fair amount of hanky-panky.' I was first reminded of the sexual underworld of cricket when World Series cricket started out in the late 1970s. Near the conclusion of a close one-day game, a camera peered into the West Indian dressing room and it caught the players relaxing with what seemed to be about a dozen white girlfriends and groupies. Once they realised a camera was beaming them into Australian living rooms there was an unedifying rush for the exit. It was from that moment that any cricketer should have realised that his private life was fair game. In the 1980s newspapers especially enjoyed reporting on the sexual conquests of Imran Khan, the handsome and haughty former Pakistani captain, who had a reputation for being a ladies' man before settling down back home in puritan Pakistan to marry the daughter of a wealthy English father. An actress friend thought he was an excellent lover. Her allegiance to men was stronger than to any one particular team, so she also bedded a famous Australian Test cricketer. 'He was not as good but had lovely shoulder blades,' she told me.

But the sexual life of cricketers on tour is not new. It's just that years before this sort of activity was never reported on. There is the story about Bill O'Reilly in the 1930s tours of England advising young players 'eager for companionship to simply follow [the spinner] Fleetwood-Smith around and talk to his castoffs'. It is said that the average cricketer contents himself with picking out one attractive woman at the innumerable functions touring teams attend. Fleetwood-Smith had no trouble slotting in four or five. A team-mate found him one night in the toilet leaning against a wash basin.' "Just resting before the next one," said Chuck.' Although O'Reilly was perplexed by Fleetwood-Smith's success: 'It was strange, as he had no line of conversation when he first met a woman. You would look on horrified at the low level of gibberish he would spray at these giggling, but well-endowed females. However, they always fell prostrate when they looked at him.' (The former school teacher probably meant supine, or else Fleetwood-Smith's female conquests were practising a foolproof method of birth control on the first date.)

It is much easier to imagine the debonair former fighter pilot Keith Miller being the centre of attention. This brilliant all-rounder, with his long black hair, square visage and cavalier approach to the game, was adored by women. As he was to say: 'I get all kinds of stuff. You know the sort of thing: "Keith, I adore you. Keith, I must see you …", all that sort of caper. Some of them send me photographs, others send trinkets, lucky charms, cuff-links and things.' And, of course, sooner or later, as with every cricketer on tour, the wives and girlfriends hear gossip and it takes a very understanding spouse to deal with this, as Miller ruefully admitted. 'The other day my picture was published in a paper alongside an Australian girl. So I quickly called the missus in Sydney and asked her if she had seen the paper. "Yes, dear," she said.

"'With a girl?'

"'Yes, dear.'

"'She was only an Australian model.'

"'Yes, dear. And if that's your story, dear, you stick to it, dear.'"

For women, young men in their twenties, fully fit, successful and well known, are an attractive proposition. For bachelors there is a large contingent of women wanting to have sex with them. Kerry O'Keefe, a leg spinner, remembered touring the West Indies and 'sitting around the swimming pool with all the single blokes watching the British Airlines planes arrive so we could pick up the hosties'. A few years later in the West Indies Roland Fishman, reporting on the Australian 1991 tour, related how one Australian Test cricketer had sex with about thirty women. For the rest of the team the term for sex was thempties. One player bragged he had had four thempties in one night. A few years ago an Australian tabloid offered evidence of a former Australian captain's fondness for gobbling down his young mistress's edible panties. Of course, this behaviour wasn't confined to the Australians.

In January, 2002 a former Test cricketer, Qasim Omar, claimed that top Pakistani players had thrown matches in return for sex with Australian prostitutes. The deals were allegedly made in hotels such as the Sheraton in Sydney, a restaurant in Kings Cross and a McDonald's in Melbourne (the conflation of junk food and junk sex has some sort of inevitability about it). According to Omar, the prostitutes included a doctor, a nurse, travel agent and television presenter and were supplied by two Sydney madams. Of the 23 prostitutes all were Australian except for one Pakistani and a Chinese woman. A few weeks after the report an Australian woman claimed she had been the late West Indian fast bowler Malcolm Marshall's girlfriend when she was fifteen. Ian Botham was attached to several sex scandals, including the beefy Englishman's strenuous sessions on a West Indies tour that resulted in a broken bed. In 2001 there were more scandals, this time the press delighting in the discovery that Botham had an Australian mistress and had 'built a love nest' Down Under where he proved to have a liking for 'bondage games'. There were photographs of the grim and preternaturally patient Mrs Botham waiting for her errant husband to return to England to explain yet another example of his misbehaviour.

According to a recent issue of the high-society magazine *Tatler*, 'Cricket has thrown off its sad old flannels and reinvented itself as a sexy game, played by beautiful people in beautiful places ... For heaven's sake, Jemima Goldsmith married a cricketer [Imran Khan] – how big a hint do you need?' As if confirmation were needed, a woman told the *Sydney Morning Herald* of how in 1995 she followed her heroes on a tour to the West Indies and before long she found herself drinking with the team and 'eight vodkas' later found herself in bed with an Australian cricketer. 'There is a code of silence,' she said. 'They are not going to dob in another guy on the team.' It was also clearly apparent to her that if you wanted to sleep with a player then it is easier to do it while they're touring. 'If you want to bag one, that's the way ... They don't know anybody ... They are away from their wives.' Jessica Halloran, the journalist who wrote the article, added: 'This is how easy it is. Stand outside the [Sydney Cricket Ground] changing rooms, ask an international sportsman for an autograph and have his signature – and telephone number – thrust back at you. Ring the telephone number and, well, let the night take you from there.' The girls who pursue sportsmen are derided as 'SCG slags' and groupies. Such women are a perk for sportsmen. One famous American basket-baller claimed he had up to 10,000 women (how he concentrated on the game seems a minor miracle). Dr Michael Martin, a sports psychologist, glumly summed up the problem: 'You mix fandom with hormones and basically this is what you are getting. Some of the higher-profile athletes are already in stable relationships and this thing can be a distraction. Prior and after performance.'

From the moment Warne became famous – and therefore fair game – the English press in particular has been obsessed by his off-field behaviour. Before he was married, the tabloids would drag out some former girl-friend or one-night stand and for a fee the women gave graphic details. Warne has always said that most of these stories were half fiction, half fact, and many pure fiction, so in 1999 when a woman announced in the English tabloid *News of the World* she had had sex with Warne in 1997 not many people took notice. Kelly Handley, a buxom porn star, said that she had 'hot sex' with Warne although she rated him only 0.5 out of ten. In the same year Warne's wife was dismayed to see a newspaper photograph of her husband on a South African cricket boundary fence signing his autograph on the buttocks of a girl who had helpfully lifted up her miniskirt for him to do so.

Not much notice was taken of Handley's allegations but in the following year, 2000, while Warne was play-ing county cricket for Hampshire, there was another allegation, this time on the front page of the *Daily Mirror* and later on television. An English nurse called Donna Smith said that Warne had left 'sex messages' on her answer machine. She sounded like the innocent party

and Warne's behaviour more like harassment than anything consensual. 'I had no idea who he was. I'm not a
cricket fan. He was really unattractive. He was podgy
and very tanned. He had dyed blond hair and I could see
the roots,' she said. The newspaper also quoted from the
answer machine recordings conveniently supplied by
Ms Smith.

For Warne the telephone sex was merely 'explicit talk
between two consenting adults' and he protested that he
had been the one who had been pursued. One night
he was in a Leicester nightclub when Smith approached
him and asked him to autograph her back, which he
refused to do. 'Then she tried to lift up my shirt and said
she would sign my body instead. I told her that was out
of order.' According to Warne she didn't go but 'kept
hanging around' and when he was leaving she told him
she was a 'very good talker on the phone'. In trying to
find an excuse Warne blamed the drink for listening
to her even though it was more than a week later when
he phoned her for telephone sex. She rang back a few
days later and they had phone sex again.

Simone Warne was also in England at the time of the
scandal and he had a lot of explaining to do, as one can
well imagine. The reader is pleased he glosses over it in
a discreet sentence in his autobiography: 'It took time
for the marriage to get back to where it was before, but
we eventually succeeded through talking and love.' The
controversy was massive, especially in Australia, and,
again, those bastions of moral rectitude, indignant sports
writers and columnists, called for him to be sacked from
the Test cricket team.

Warne avoided the press and went on television, where the questions were easier. He tried to talk his way out of the crisis but didn't sound convincing. He may have shared a liking for telephone sex with the former American President but he doesn't have Bill Clinton's ability to see language as having a plasticine malleability that makes meaning merely something to be moulded in an infinite variety of ways that have nothing to do with the truth. He could not squirm his way out of the fact that he had had telephone sex, and there were no excuses he could fall back on. Realising that many critics wanted Warne dumped, even though the incident had nothing to do with his job as cricketer, the ACB, in the person of Malcolm Speed, the chief executive, met him in London and presented him with a book of Australian newspaper articles and files on the incident. Warne was gobsmacked to see that it was several hundred pages long. Speed agreed that the incident had been blown out of proportion but the majority of the fourteen directors on the Board were still angry at what Warne had done. A short time later he was stripped of his vice-captaincy, a decision that hurt him acutely. He had lost his position because of what he regarded as purely a private matter: 'Explicit talk on the telephone did not mean that all of a sudden I'd lost my flipper or forgotten how to set a field.' Admitting he had made a mistake is something Warne rarely likes to do, but he did this time because he so much wanted to captain Australia. His position is simple: 'I have given my heart and soul to Australian cricket and I like to think I have earned the respect of the ACB. I have helped to put a few backsides on seats and made spin bowling more interesting. I play in an aggressive, animated, emotional way which reflects the pride I take in representing my country. That should have counted for something I would have thought.'

But it didn't, because times had changed and Warne hadn't noticed. The public image of sportsmen was becoming of paramount importance, whether it be a footballer or cricketer. The marketing of sports meant that its heroes, or at least their public image, had to be what was termed 'a cleanskin'. All Warne had to do was witness the public humiliation and fall of one of the greatest Australian Rules footballers of the past decade. After being forgiven by his club for several incidents which included indecently assaulting a young woman, sexually harassing another (though the club paid her to be quiet) he was forced to leave the North Melbourne team after having an affair with a team-mate's wife. Warne's failure to realise how perceptions of private and public behaviour are coupled in the contemporary public's eye, and reinforced by a prurient and prying media is easy to see in his quaint identification with the character of the Fonz in the American sit-com *Happy Days*. As far as he's concerned what the Australian Test team doesn't need as captain is someone 'squeaky clean' like the character Richie Cunningham 'who was always polite and well-mannered, who said the right things at the right times, but relied on the Fonz, a more confident, streetwise figure, to overcome his problems in the real world.'

And indeed he is entitled to feel a little aggrieved

when he looks at the career of the present one-day captain Ricky Ponting, a fervent punter who has been
involved in several grubby and very public episodes,
including one in India where the drunken Tasmanian
groped and made unwelcome advances to several
women at a club and when rejected made coarse gestures towards his penis. When he was ejected he soon
returned and was quickly caught up in another scuffle.
Back in Australia there was another incident, this time at
the Bourbon and Beefsteak Bar in Kings Cross where in
the early hours of the morning, drunk again, he groped
and fondled women until finally a large Maori security
guard put a stop to his gross behaviour with what Warne
would call 'a knuckle sandwich'. The next day the pictures of a drunken Ponting outside the Bourbon and
Beefsteak, sporting a black eye, were on the front pages
of daily newspapers. Ponting was forced to make a
humiliating confession of his drink problem at a press
conference, but these incidents have apparently been
forgiven.

However, Warne could not stay out of the papers. He
has an unrivalled knack for creating unintentional publicity. Just after arriving in South Africa on the 2002 tour
newspapers reported on another incident, this time
involving two teenage girls and an attempt at extortion
after the uncle of one of the girls alleged that Shane
Warne and team-mate Brett Lee had made suggestive
comments to the pair in January, 2002. The uncle called
the ACB, wanting $5000 and tickets to matches in
exchange for not telling the media. According to the
girls one of the men tongue-kissed her and asked her to

show him her breasts. Both Lee and Warne dismissed the claims as 'rubbish'. The ACB quickly investigated the matter and found that following a one-day match in Brisbane, the cricketers drove to the Gold Coast, intending to visit a casino. They were followed by three people in a car including a sixteen-year-old girl. The ACB investigator found that Warne only allowed the girl to kiss him on the cheek in a bid to stop them following their car. Five people were questioned over the matter by police and one man was arrested over the blackmail allegations at Melbourne airport. Tim May, Warne's former spin partner and now head of the International Players' Union, said that such events 'highlighted the increasing number of off-field pressures which confronted all top-level sportspeople'. He went on to say that Australian cricket was trying to promote greater awareness of 'the pitfalls awaiting careless players. But inevitably, the responsibility lay with individuals who needed to recognise and avoid damaging scenarios before they arose'.

Warne has failed to grasp the advice and if there is a common theme through the increasingly murky plot lines of his personal soap opera it is that he seldom thinks of the consequences of his actions, which is why he probably thinks of himself as the spontaneous, 'streetwise' Fonz. Among many examples that relate to cricket there is the result of his abiding dislike of the squat, rotund and argumentative Sri Lankan captain, Arjuna Ranatunga. The Sri Lankan proved himself an excellent leader. His team won the 1996 World Cup against the Australians, but he boorishly refused to shake the hands of his defeated opponents at the end of the game. His abrasive manner was born out of a belief that colonialism still existed in the cricket world. This belief drove him to deliberately annoy and pester white cricketers, an attitude that was stunningly successful – most white cricketers loathed him. When not protecting his off spin bowler Muttiah Muralitharan from being no-balled for illegal deliveries by trying to browbeat the umpires, he was threatening to walk off grounds when decisions went against his team. He had a contemptuous attitude towards Australians and a small man's querulous aggression that was later to have him arrested for assault soon after he retired from cricket. What galled Warne was that Ranatunga never made him forget how badly the leg spinner bowled during the 1996 final. Once when asked about the Australian leg spinner he sniffily dismissed him as 'an over-hyped creation of the media'. Naturally inventive at finding excuses, Warne blamed his poor display in 1996 on the ball being difficult to grasp in the dewy conditions. During the early days of the 1999 World Cup in England, just after he had been named by Wisden as one of the three most influential cricketers of the modern era (the other two members of the triumvirate were Viv Richards and Ian Botham), Warne opined in *The Times* that Ranatunga's sullen aggressiveness and coarse gamesmanship were bad for the game as a whole and Sri Lankan cricket in particular and as such he shouldn't be playing in the tournament.

Of course Ranatunga found Warne's comments inflammatory. However, he easily won the verbal duel by responding with the acid observation about Warne and Australian culture: 'We come from 2500 years of culture and we know where [the Australians] come from.' The not-too-subtle dig at our convict heritage infuriated Warne, but what annoyed him even more was that he was fined for his own comment and given a two-match suspended sentence while the Sri Lankan didn't even get a reprimand. What Warne had forgotten was that contracts for the competition quite clearly stated that no player should say anything derogatory about other players. Again the controversy was on the front pages and again Warne felt his familiar mixture of hurt and bewilderment and a sense that he had been picked on. His resentment still runs deep and he defends his actions: 'Some people are so worried about appearing politically correct and saying all the right things that they never express what they really think. It seems a strange society when you cannot express an opinion.' He's probably right, but he still has trouble understanding that his enormous profile means he has to be more careful than probably any other cricketer in the world about what he says and does. It may be unfair, but that's the position he finds himself in.

Even embroiled in cricket controversies and sexual misdemeanours he was on the way to becoming a wealthy man, who was supported by many generous sponsors. An estimated 70 per cent of his income comes from such deals. Nike and Just Jeans were two important sponsors, but it was a deal with Nicorette that was to result in more headlines. A long-time smoker, he was approached by the company at a time when he wanted to give up, especially as his non-smoking wife ordered him outside every time he wanted a puff. The firm promoted a chewing gum infused with small amounts of nicotine which they believe helps to wean people off cigarettes. Warne was offered around $200,000 to endorse the product and be a living testament to its properties by undertaking the program. Because he was such a public figure his struggle – and they hoped ultimate success – in curing himself of his addiction would vindicate investing so much money in him. Warne told them that he was strong willed enough to succeed. Here the company might well have paused and asked itself just how much willpower he had shown off the field, but apparently not. The deal caused much media comment and it was easy for a reporter to find a few whingers who moaned about the fact that they weren't being given such a financial incentive to stop smoking.

Warne and his manager tried to reverse this sort of negative publicity with a deliberate policy of courting and stroking reporters. He took half a dozen of the most significant cricket writers to a restaurant at one of his favourite Melbourne places – the Crown Casino – and over a long lunch, while he puffed away, enjoying what he hoped would be his last cigarettes, he tried to charm his critics. What he and his manager failed to grasp was that such an event only massaged the egos of the journalists. After the effects of the alcohol and the charm offensive had dissipated like smoke rings, the brittle relationship had hardly changed at all.

Warne started his non-smoking regimen in January, 1999 and seemed to be making good progress, but by early April he was dropped from the team to play the West Indies in the fourth and final Test in Antigua. The disappointment gnawed at him and during the celebrations after Australia won without him all it needed was a few beers for his resolve to break. He has the uncanny ability to do the wrong thing at the right time for others with a mercenary impulse, and it wasn't long before a man took the opportunity to photograph him smoking and, jumping around with delight, kept shouting out: 'I'm going to sell this!' And he was as good as his word.

The publicity was immense and there was much smirking commentary on Warne's lack of determination. Nicorette forgave their wayward representative but were sorely tested when during the 1999 World Cup Warne, blaming the pressure, was smoking again. He says he did not intend to mislead Nicorette but the expensive sponsorship was an all-too-public lack of success which said little for his willpower. Still irritated years later, he tried to downplay his failure: 'Really [it wasn't] an issue of national importance, but the media kept on harping about it.' It never seemed to occur to him that by taking such a huge amount of money to stop smoking he was inviting everyone to publicly evaluate the success of the experiment, that even then he was probably on a hiding to nothing, because if he had stopped smoking permanently the media and the public would have thought that for such a large amount of money anyone could give up. It's not facetious to say that one of Warne's admirable traits is always to see that the glass is half full not half empty. He saw the experiment as having the positive outcome of reducing his daily intake of forty-five cigarettes to twenty. Relinquishing the sponsorship meant that a few years later in the exciting conclusion to the crucial Second Test against South Africa in 2002, as a nervous Warne waited to bat he could puff away on a cigarette in full public gaze without feeling guilty.

Warne was again to find himself in strife because of his smoking. In February, 2000 he played a one-day game against New Zealand in Wellington in a new stadium that had been declared smoke free and as such anyone who was caught smoking could be fined up to NZ$10,000. Apparently an official told Warne that he could smoke if he kept it to the privacy of the dressing-room. But the official's rule proved too subtle for Warne and during a rain break he was smoking outside in front of the dressing-room while playing cards with several others. Without warning there was a camera flash and for Warne there was a feeling of *déjà vu* as he turned around to see two teenage boys whooping with delight, one of them crowing 'We've got a picture!'

There are conflicting reports of what happened next. According to Warne he thought he'd let the matter pass but after the card game finished he approached the boys and asked them why they wanted the picture. There is no doubt that he dreaded more publicity about his smoking and the fact that he had seriously compromised a helpful official and could himself be fined NZ$10,000. He presented the two boys with a compromise. If they gave him the disposable camera he would have the film developed and give them all the shots except for the one of him smoking. The boys agreed but said they wanted to use up the rest of the film photographing the New Zealand players, and said they would give the Australian the camera after the game. Because of rain the game finished early and Warne went in search of the camera. The boys said the camera had been stolen and when Warne didn't believe them they offered their bag for him to frisk. Of course the camera wasn't there and Warne kept the bag, offering to trade it for the camera. As can only happen to Warne, soon, all too soon, things escalated out of control. A man appeared demanding the cricketer give back the bag and then a policeman turned up and he also demanded that he give back the bag. Warne did and much to his chagrin the policeman told the boys that they hadn't broken any laws and were free to go. When Warne protested, the policeman, thoroughly enjoying Warne's discomfort, remarked sarcastically: 'Why don't you have another cigarette and I'll take your picture as well?'

The next step in this saga is easily predictable. Andy Warhol was nearly right in saying that in the future everyone will be famous for fifteen minutes. What he forgot to say was that everyone will be desperate to be famous for fifteen minutes. The publicity was stupendous. The policeman got his name and his version of the event in the newspapers, the two boys went on television saying that Warne used to be a hero of theirs but he was no longer after he had sworn at them and attempted to steal their bag. The murky aura of being no more than a common crook settled on Warne. When back in Wellington for a Test match, he helped arrange for the boys to attend and then had a chat with them where he apologised and, according to Warne, both teenagers said the media had hounded them into talking about the incident.

But before he could relax into believing that the matter was over, the boys popped up on television again, saying the Australian wasn't apologetic at all. To Warne this was further confirmation that he wasn't able to control his own destiny. He felt like he was merely part of a preordained script as predictable as any generic Hollywood movie. As he could say with experience: 'The first stories, blown-up with big headlines, are usually the most damaging and once again my reputation had suffered before the truth emerged, but sometimes mud sticks …' And it did, especially in New Zealand, whose fixation with the bigger, more arrogant Australia is almost a national obsession, probably made worse by the fact that so many New Zealanders want to work and live here. 'If there was any misunderstanding, I do apologise,' said Warne after the incident. He probably thought that he was safe from controversy within the confines of the cricket oval but then he found himself caught up in one, this time involving a team-mate.

In late 1999 when the Second Test against Pakistan had been won by Australia after a remarkable partnership between the mollydookers, Justin Langer and Adam Gilchrist, Warne became a victim of a piece of mischievous observation by members of *The Panel*, a Channel 10 talk show based on the cheaply produced but successful idea of bringing half a dozen people together, as if friends at a dinner party, to chatter about what's in the news. Sometimes sharply funny, the members of the panel can lapse into smarmy and self-congratulatory laughter at their own cleverness. Notoriously prickly at even the most minor of criticisms, the company that produces and partakes in the show is nevertheless not shy to dish out criticism. *The Panel* obtained footage of the Test match and after fiddling with the audio picked up a voice saying of Warne's team-mate Scott Muller's particularly clumsy piece of fielding off the leg spinner's bowling: 'Can't bowl, can't throw.'

What followed was something that became a harrowing episode for Warne, because all too quickly newspapers and the public decided that it was he who had said the words. He struggled to try to contain what he knew in his heart was going to be a controversy. Muller had been dropped from the Test team but according to Warne had previously told the leg spinner that he was the 'only one who went out of his way to make him feel welcome'. So it seemed that the Queenslander would believe his innocence even if the ravenous press didn't. Warne rang Muller, who was beside himself with fury and paranoia. He cursed the astonished Warne, accused him of pretending to be a friend, and believed that the leg spinner was lying. Warne, who has a horror of being disliked by any team-mate, as he has an old-fashioned but fierce belief in the redeeming power and inherent strengths of mateship, actively sought out proof that he wasn't the culprit.

He asked Channel 9 to examine the footage. It was discovered that there was a front-on shot in which Warne remained silent throughout the whole incident.

A close scrutiny of other angles and microphones revealed that a special effects microphone had picked up what might have been a cameraman on the boundary saying of Muller: 'He can't bowl and he can't throw.' It was the proof Warne needed and he rang Muller, only to have him stubbornly insist that the spinner was spinning a yarn.

The more Warne protested his innocence, the more he was disbelieved and the more the controversy escalated. Channel 9, Warne's employers, hunted down the culprit and produced the cameraman. Curiously they wouldn't give him a surname. Known only as 'Joe', he was exhibited on television, where he duly owned up to being the guilty party and apologised to Muller and Warne. If the leg spinner thought this was the end of the saga, he was mistaken. Joe had worn a T-shirt with the brand name Nike on it when making his apology. As Warne was sponsored by Nike, it seemed that Warne had used Joe's confession to promote the firm. Whichever way he turned he was pilloried and disbelieved. A journalist, determined to prove that it was Warne's voice on the tape, went to a voice specialist who confirmed that it wasn't Warne. Surely, thought Warne, this was the ultimate vindication that he was innocent. Yet this third and final phone call to Muller achieved nothing. The hapless and paranoiac Muller was even more convinced it was his former team-mate's voice. If that wasn't enough, when Warne next played at Muller's home ground in Brisbane the crowd booed and jeered the spinner. If anything, the affair showed how the continuing soap opera of his life had caused people to think he was capable of saying such a thing and lying about it. Like the character of Fonz, with whom he identifies, the public expected Warne to be the cause of scandal and controversy and thought of him as guilty even when he was proved innocent.

Several incidents Warne has been involved in were trivial but they became controversies not only because of his fame and celebrity but because he seems to lack an awareness of the consequences of his actions. As far as he is concerned, cause-and-effect is as mysterious a notion as the chaos theory, where a butterfly flapping its wings in the Amazon causes a hurricane in the Indian Ocean. He is aware that the writers of the soap opera he has found himself in, who twist and distort him and put him through all manner of tribulations, are frequently to be found in newspaper offices. Yet this knowledge doesn't seem to affect his behaviour. For the writers he is a perfect protagonist because, like many famous sportsmen when they are off the field, he seems to have all the self-awareness of a careless and unthinking boy in an adult's body.

10: The Comeback Kid

Allan Border once said he could hardly remember anything about his one-day match career. Modern cricketers play an inordinate amount of what used to be disparagingly called the 'pajama game'. It is a different type of cricket from Test cricket, which is one of the most coded and ceremonial of games where the subtle strategies and arcane rituals can be enjoyed for themselves. Time in Test cricket is measured out in days, not hours, and the tempo of a game can vary from fast pace to as languid as a slow-moving tide drifting in and out. One-day cricket has no memory. The game may be action-packed and instantly entertaining but the huge majority of games are forgotten by spectators and players immediately they are over. In contrast Test cricket is shored up by memories of previous great innings or bowling achievements or information so arcane that one can be overwhelmed by the minutiae. The one-day game attracts larger crowds, more boisterous and aggressive than those that attend Test cricket, and it is more appealing to television viewers, who do not want to see the subtle ebb and flow of a game but coarse batting and frantic finishes.

One-day cricket may have its detractors but it has helped transform Test cricket. Tests that would once have dawdled along for five days can now be over in three, with runs scored at a rate that matches one-day games. Probably at no other time in Test cricket has the Australian team scored at such a high rate of runs per ball. Still, one-day games have a more immediate appeal, especially as entertainment, which is why publishers put Warne on their book covers dressed not in cricket whites but in the garish yellow and green one-day colours. One-day games also allow Warne to indulge in his love of showmanship, knowing he is playing to excitable crowds. Warne is quite forthright about this, agreeing with Ian Botham, an English cricketer whose fame and controversies once matched his, that cricketers are part of the entertainment industry. Like every other élite cricketer, Warne knows it is Test cricket that reveals your talent, temperament and ability to withstand pressure. But when he arrived in England to play in the 1999 World Cup, it was the one-day game he had to turn to in order to salvage his career after having been dropped from the Test team against the West Indies.

As usual he was the centre of media attention, but the pure, unadulterated love the media had felt for him during his first tour of England had changed. The controversies and his larrikin behaviour were perfect for the tabloids to exploit, and there was also an envy of Warne's genius as a cricketer and a growing sense that he should be brought down a peg or two. Over the years he had tried to inure himself to fat gibes, which included a tabloid photo sting of a cute girl approaching Warne with a plate of party pies, double entendre headlines like 'Shane Can't Grip His Balls' when he had trouble gripping the slightly different English cricket ball and, of course, revelations of sex and illegal betting scandals and photographs of him smoking.

Despite all this, Warne has a special fondness for England and tried to charm the media, but it wanted England to win the World Cup and was prepared to criticise him as much as it could. The press knew he was under pressure because of poor form and it was thought that his shoulder had not recovered. Some openly speculated that the leg spinner was washed-up. Even he was doubting his ability to rise to the occasion and used the media to talk about his self-doubts, although a moment later in a wild mood swing he was voicing his supreme confidence. Just as he has used the media at the beginning of a tour to announce a new 'mystery' ball to bewilder his opponents, so he continued to use the media, as celebrities do, as a way of sharing inner confidences.

But deep down he was unsure if he could return to his former glories. His comeback against England a few months before where he took Mark Butcher's wicket in his opening over had proved to be a disastrous fluke, disastrous because it seemed to confirm to everyone, including Warne himself, that he had made a successful comeback. After having to sack him from the Test team, Steve Waugh was worried about whether Warne's shoulder had recovered or would ever do so. From the beginning of the World Cup series his bowling was highly erratic and it seemed open season to jeer and boo and mock him. Over the years the abuse had become worse and more obscene. The so-called 'Barmy Army' (a group of English supporters who liked to show off their scrawny torsos burnt lobster-red by the Australian sun and whose lager-fuelled abuse, both of the opposition players and their own when playing badly, which means much of the time, is sometimes entertaining but mostly tedious) sang songs about Warne like: 'There's only one Shane Warne/There's only one Shane Warne/with his little bag of sweets/and his cheeky smile/Warnie is an Aussie paedophile' or 'Five men went to bed/Went to bed with Shane Warne/Five men, four men, three men, two men/one man and his sheep – Baa!/Went to bed with Shane Warne.' Other spectators openly abused him and others wore T-shirts that said 'Bog Off Fat Boy'. In 1997 Steve Waugh had stopped a minor county game in Taunton when he thought the abuse of Warne had gone 'beyond a joke'. In the same year David Hopps wrote of an Edgbaston crowd savagely abusing Warne: 'They could hardly have been more partisan with Warne copping the boos, the ridicule and derisive songs.' In his diary of the World Cup series Waugh was again struck by the way Warne was treated, even off the field when out having a drink in a pub with his team-mates: 'Seven or eight of the boys went out for a drink and mixed with some lively Scots. Their chants filled the pub and were good fun to listen to, although they did give Warney a bit of stick. But this seems par for the course in England. He has a genuine "love-hate" relationship with the Poms.' To a team-mate like Langer the English crowd's treatment of the spinner could be downright horrible: 'I would shudder if my daughter, my wife, my mum or my grandmother had to listen to the disgusting and thoughtless rubbish coming from the stands.' But sometimes Warne is unaware of the content of the abuse and at one ground he thought the crowd was chanting *'Shane Warne is a real bloke'*. An English journalist had to tell him they were saying *'Shane Warne is a rent boy'*. 'Oh,' said a puzzled Warne. 'Is that good or bad?'

It was not only the English who baited him. During an early World Cup match against Scotland the spectators were unrelenting in their vituperation, with one group showing off a huge inflatable whale which, they crowed, resembled him. Waugh thought it unfair that his spinner had to put up with the constant abuse. Warne finally broke and 'gave them the bird', an action that Waugh correctly surmised in that night's diary entry would 'make the papers tomorrow, under a big anti-Warne headline, which will be a real distortion of what went on'. What Warne saw as light-hearted interplay with the crowd, the media saw as gross and boorish behaviour.

Australia stumbled, losing early games in the tournament. Warne's bowling came in for increasing criticism. Against India he was clubbed for 49 runs in six overs with one over costing 21 runs. Waugh was beginning to realise he had a problem. That night after the match he wrote in his diary: 'I can understand, after what happened today, why some people are suggesting that

Shane's merely a very good bowler now, but not the great bowler he used to be. I can sense that some [of the other] teams are treating him like that, too, I think …'
He tried to assure himself that it would be wrong to write off a player he regarded as 'the greatest spin bowler in the history of the game' but seemed less than convinced.

Off the field there was the Ranatunga affair and Kelly Handley, the porn star, who revealed in a tabloid that the affair with Warne, started in 1997, had continued, only now they were having phone sex: 'He went mad listening to me. You could hear him going wild.' The revelations, plus the fact that Simone was about to give birth to their second son, plus his poor bowling were weighing heavily on Warne. 'Warney is a concern to all of us at the moment,' Waugh wrote. 'He's been a bit quiet, as if the pressures and hassles of the past fortnight have worn him down.' Indeed they had, and it showed in the next game against Zimbabwe, a cricketing nation so young that Australia was yet to play a Test against it. Warne grabbed a solitary wicket but proved very expensive, with one batsman hitting him for four fours in an over.

His bowling performance, plus the media's criticism of it, the scandals and controversies of the past couple of years, had finally worn him down. Overwhelmed by events and profoundly depressed, he told the Australian team the next day that he was going to retire. The team didn't know if he meant immediately or after the tournament. A concerned Waugh took the leg spinner for a long walk in Hyde Park. Warne confided in his captain probably as he had never done outside his family. He was thoroughly exhausted by the almost daily controversies and the criticisms: 'I felt that I was having to justify myself all the time. I acknowledged that I brought some of the problems on myself, but that did not ease my frustrations. I told Steve that enough was enough. Plain and simple. In a nutshell I was ready to quit.' Warne's decision to retire was no momentary aberration and the Australian captain was surprised by his combination of vehemence, hurt and plain emotional exhaustion. They discussed his sporting future and his options. Waugh wanted him to play out the tournament, go back to Australia and, after discussing it with his family, then make a decision. After returning from the park Waugh was uncertain about the effect of his words on the spinner: 'To be honest,' he wrote, 'I really don't know which way Warney's going to go. It might depend on how he bowls tomorrow against South Africa and then, if we get through, how he goes for the rest of the tournament.' The problem for Australia was that they had begun the World Cup series so badly that they had to win all of their last seven games to take the trophy. Every game was crucial. And what the Australians needed was for their deeply troubled spinner to start performing.

Waugh was pinning his hopes on the fact that Warne would be bowling against Daryll Cullinan the next day and if any batsman was going to force Warne to rise to the occasion it would be his perennial victim. Soon Australia was in a desperate plight, because after scoring a mediocre 213, the South African opening batsmen were no wicket for 45 after only nine overs. Waugh could see that none of his fast bowlers was capable of slowing down the scoring and, given the brazen start by the openers, he knew that the only way to achieve this was to take wickets. He looked around the field and, spotting Warne, realised that he was the side's only hope. So in desperation Waugh threw him the ball. If Warne were the true champion Waugh believed he was, then now was the time to deliver. It was a moment that Warne was to recall with a tinge of bitterness, as the disappointment at being dropped from the Test team still rankled: 'It was strange to think that my argument about being the man to perform when it mattered had cut no ice in the West Indies two months earlier.'

Warne was nervous and continually licked his dry lips. As he was to remark afterwards: 'It was do or die time. I had to know, under pressure, whether I could do it or not.' He was bowling to Herschelle Gibbs and not long into his spell he bowled a ball that began heading towards leg stump and then seemed to drift even further outside the right-hander's leg side and Gibbs prodded forward, in as correct a defensive movement as you could ever expect to see. The ball landed and then, suddenly, as if having hit an invisible wall, it cut back and turned so dramatically that it hit the off stump. It was a ball as good as 'the ball of the century' and, like Gatting, Gibbs stared at the shattered wicket and back down at the bowler, as if what Warne had done was impossible. But Warne paid no attention to the bemused batsman. He was screaming to himself and his team, 'Come on! Come on!' Warne was rejuvenated by the wicket. 'Hang on a minute,' he remembers thinking, 'I can still turn the ball a long way.'

As I watched this on television in the early hours of an Australian morning, I knew I had to stay up and see the game to its conclusion. There was something about Warne's startling transformation that boded well. His body language quickly changed from someone hoping to get a wicket to someone who was determined to get a wicket every ball. He seemed to pulsate with the excitement and energy of expectation.

The sight of Warne spinning the ball so much and so early in his bowling spell greatly affected the waiting batsmen in the South African dressing-room. They became defensive and uncertain in their stroke play, which was to help account for Warne's next wicket in his second over. Worried that Warne was beginning to mentally dominate, the other opener, Gary Kirsten, decided to belt Warne out of the attack. It was a pre-meditated decision to whack the ball to the leg-side boundary but it's always a dubious move to make up your mind before the ball is bowled, given that Warne's deliveries have so many variables. Warne threw the ball up outside the left-hander's off stump, Kirsten gave an almighty swing at it, a shot of determination and blind wilfulness, but failed to connect. A split-second later he heard the ball rattle his stumps. Kirsten's dismissal galvanised Warne. He swung his arms wildly, his eyes rolled and he was screaming at the sky and then at his fellow players: 'Come on! Come on!' His reaction had a similar intensity to his send-off of Hudson a few years earlier, only this wasn't directed at the batsman. It was an inner eruption directed at no-one in particular: it was an inarticulate purging of a fetid mire of stored-up real and imagined slights and bitter resentments and public humiliation. It was as if a pressure cooker had exploded open after being unlocked by success. It all poured out: the recent failures, being dropped, sex scandals, the irritating Ranatunga, the paranoiac Muller, the persistent and obscene abuse of the crowds, missing the birth of his child, the perception that he was washed-up, the public sniggering over the controversies, the moralistic press, and his own profound doubts about his talent and his ability to come back. He was like a man possessed and had to tell himself to calm down. He took deep rasping breaths, trying to find his composure and refocus on the game. He had overcome and purged his demons in the one place that mattered, the one place where he could control his destiny and could confront his enemies. In one of the most important games he had ever played he had faced a frightening and foul darkness inside himself and had found cathartic release.

The next over Warne had Cronje, caught at first slip. The captain, who, as usual, had arrived grim-faced, departed with a face screwed up in misery (not such an overreaction when replays showed the ball probably hit his toe and not the bat). At the end of eight overs Warne had taken three wickets for twelve runs. The game was now in the balance. Cullinan seemed to decide that if he couldn't get out to the leg spinner he would run himself out and promptly did so. By the time Warne came back for his final two overs, South Africa needed to pick up the tempo or else it would run out of overs. Warne bowled steadily during his ninth and in the tenth found himself being hit for a two, six and a four off the first three balls, valuable runs that gave South Africa a good chance of victory. Pollock's audacious counter-attack seem to momentarily unhinge Warne: 'My eyes started spinning. I was so fired up I had to calm myself down.' The next ball was a single and so Kallis now faced Warne. Nothing was scored off the next ball. For the final ball of his allotted ten overs Warne realised he must not allow his emotions to get the better of him. He took a deep breath as he paused at the top of his run-up. He then bowled what looked like a standard leg break with not too much turn. Kallis aimed his shot through the off side, but Warne had held back the ball and it was slower than the previous delivery. By the time Kallis was through with the shot he realised he was too early on it and he sliced it to Steve Waugh for a simple catch. So easily did Kallis seem to capitulate that the dismissal was underrated, but really it revealed just how subtle, thoughtful and delicate was Warne's bowling in the intense heat of the contest. It was a remarkable achievement for a man under such pressure.

It seemed as though Warne's four wickets, which his captain thought to be one of the greatest bowling spells in international one-day cricket history, had sealed victory for Australia but the South African all-rounder Klusener assaulted the bowling in a brutal manner that caused, as Warne was to write, 'the famous Australian self-belief to seep away.' A dropped catch and a dismal attempt at a run-out meant that with three balls to go the scores were level and South Africa needed only one

run and Australia one wicket to win. The noise of the
crowd was so loud that the players could barely hear one
another even if they shouted. The pressure on both
teams was intense and fierce because the winner would
go into the final against Pakistan. Both Klusener and his
partner, Donald, had the bright glazed eyes of unimaginable inner anxiety and agitation. If he had been
clear-headed Klusener would have realised he had a precious three balls to score the solitary run but when he
saw the next ball from Fleming was going to be pitched
right up to him, a length he particularly liked, he swung
firmly but mishit and the ball dribbled away. Muddle-
headed with tension and the desperate desire to win, he
set off for an impossible run. Startled on seeing his partner hurrying down the wicket, and remembering all too
clearly the near run-out in the previous over, Donald
stepped back to the safety of his own crease, probably
hoping that Klusener would turn and scurry back to his
own crease, but he didn't and so Donald, now riven by
panic, dropped his bat and scurried down the pitch in a
forlorn attempt to beat the ball, which had been picked
up by Mark Waugh, who then threw it to Fleming near
the bowler's end, and who, despite the hysterical cries of
his team-mates yelling 'Keeper's end! Keeper's end!'
calmly rolled the ball to wicket-keeper Gilchrist as
Donald, seemingly all arms and legs like a scarecrow
caught in the wind of his own panic, saw the ball race
ahead of him along the pitch. A long way from the
safety of the crease he could only watch the Australian
keeper take off the bails. It was a tie which confused
the captain, who yelled out at Warne as they ran off the

ground, 'Are we in? Are we in?' 'We're in, mate, you beauty,' shouted back Warne. Because of their superior run rate during the tournament, they were in the final.

Warne won the man-of-the-match award and won it again in the final where Australia easily beat Pakistan and he, now bowling with that familiar arrogant confidence, took four wickets. Waugh realised it was his leg spinner who had put them in the finals: 'If I had to pinpoint one moment that got us through, it would have to be *that* ball ... the one from Warney that rocked Herschelle Gibbs.' It was a ball every bit as defining as Warne's 'ball of the century'. Warne's comeback had been spectacular. In the most exciting one-day international ever played, he had fought a battle with himself and his detractors and won. He had silenced his doubters and his own doubts, for the time being at least.

11: The Australian Ethos

After his efforts in the World Cup Warne decided he had four or five years of Test cricket left in him and the selectors duly chose him. Back in Australia the State selectors were not so kind and he was dumped as the captain of Victoria. This had nothing to do with his misdemeanours. His time as Victorian captain was notable for its lack of success. Just as his bowling career in District and State cricket is mediocre so was his captaincy. Warne thrives on big occasions and larger audiences than those two competitions can provide.

He had a successful tour of Sri Lanka, proving he was now back at his best, but Australia lost the rain-affected series and then won a one-off Test match against Zimbabwe, little knowing that the inaugural Test against the new cricket nation was to be the start of the most successful run of victories ever in Test cricket; a phenomenal string of sixteen consecutive victories of which Warne was an essential part. Led by new captain,

Steve Waugh, the Australian team mirrored his ruthless approach and harsh confidence. They played dynamic and exhilarating cricket, blending the attacking style of one-day cricket with the remorseless concentration required of Test cricket. Unlike the overrated 1948 so-called Invincibles, who were centred on the genius of Don Bradman and defeated a war-exhausted English team, Waugh's band had an amazing ability to find the right player for the occasion. The strength of the team was in the team spirit itself. If one batsman failed, then another stepped in to retrieve the situation. If one player was dropped because of illness or lack of form then the replacement – of whom there seemed an unlimited supply – came into the team and immediately proved himself. Sentiment was not enough to remain in the Test Eleven. The exceptional wicket-keeper Ian Healy was dropped, even though he was desperate to play a final Test in front of his home crowd in Brisbane. His replacement Adam Gilchrist entered the team in a seam-less succession and went on to play some of the most magnificent and entertaining innings in the history of Test cricket. Michael Slater, whose batting average was formidably good for an opener, but whose footwork in the 2001 Ashes resembled a chook dancing on a hot plate, was replaced by Justin Langer, who had previously been dropped, and Langer, grasping his opportunity, realising it was all too easy to be replaced, developed an opening partnership with another cack-hander, Matthew Hayden, that was amazingly productive and thrilling to watch. If anyone summed up the team motto it was Langer: 'Never take the baggy green cap for granted, because you never know when the last time you are going to wear it is going to be.'

In Tests against Pakistan, then India in Australia, Warne was back to his best. He was even able to exact the occasional revenge on his nemesis, Tendulkar, and in New Zealand he passed Dennis Lillee's record number of wickets (355) as the greatest Australian wicket taker. If his bowling didn't win as many Test matches as before, it didn't particularly matter. Waugh had developed his unit not as a collection of individuals but as a team, infused with a collective spirit, a spirit that was deliberately and, on occasions, obnoxiously Australian.

Waugh's emphasis on collective responsibility and self-belief as a team was in the great Australian tradition. As Allan Border wrote about the pedigree of Waugh's team: 'One characteristic that has often distinguished Australian teams has been the commitment to the team cause. Other teams often give the impression they are a group of individuals pulled together by selectors and they could split apart at any time. The Indians are often like that. It cannot be easy when you have three different languages being spoken on the field with some players not understanding others.' Warne has said approvingly of the team ethos: 'Anybody [in the team] who becomes too big for his boots is quickly cut down to size.' And he enthusiastically agrees with Waugh who as captain deliberately moulded what he called 'a team without stars'. 'That might seem an odd thing to write,' he reflected in his 2001 diary, 'given that we have players of the calibre of Glenn McGrath, Shane Warne and Adam Gilchrist, especially as all three took the plaudits during our Ashes-retaining victory. But our belief is that any sustained success has to be based on the combined efforts of the team rather than relying time and again on the same individuals.'

From the beginning of the game in Australia cricket has been tied up with the national identity. Simon Caterson, in an article called 'Towards a Cricket History of Australia', theorises that 'for European Australians, the purpose of cricket was never merely recreation. The newly historicised cricket was introduced into Australia at a time that proved propitious, since it provided the basis for the establishment of the new society. The obvious illustration is Victoria. Not only is the Melbourne Cricket Club the oldest surviving cricket club in Australia, it is the oldest institution of any kind in Victoria.'

Since 1877 when Test cricket started in Australia the national team has carried with it a larger burden than merely the game itself. As Warne has said, since an early age it's 'beaten into Australians that they have to beat the Poms'. As a colonial country with a hazy sense of itself, defeating their English masters at cricket had a profound resonance for Australians. It not only gave a clear-cut demonstration of superiority, it provided the English with an easily absorbed image of its colony; a land of fit young men, of boundless opportunity, of a country that could breed wonderful sportsmen because of diet, sunshine and a classless system.

In beating the Mother Country the Australian team demonstrated the virtues of its powerful sentiment that the basis of the national identity was mateship. Cricket was the great leveller and one man's deeds were never to be extolled over those of the team itself, which is why Don Bradman never indulged in 'big-noting' himself. His efforts were appreciated of course, but his identity had to be swallowed up in the national sense of self. If he had become larger than the Australian team's concept of itself then he would have been ostracised. As it was, some of the other players were irritated at the way he didn't conform to this identity off the field. Instead of drinking and socialising with his team-mates he spent his free time by himself, an act which went strongly against the concept of mateship.

By playing against England, Australia was also confirming its British heritage. The rules and regulations and the notion of fair play were invented by the English and even though Australians loved beating them, there was no Republican spirit to it. The English were still the arbitrators of what constituted cricket, social graces, art and education. Politics truly entered the world of cricket during the early 1930s when the English captain Jardine developed the Leg Theory or Bodyline, a tactic to combat the brilliance of Bradman. The tactic used bouncers deliberately aimed at the batsman so if he were not hit then he defended himself with the bat and in all likelihood the ball would be hit into the air on the leg side, which was packed with catchers. The tactic caused injuries and was regarded as unfair or *just not cricket*. The situation for the Australians was summed up by their captain Bill Woodfull who famously remarked: 'There are two sides out there. One is trying to play cricket, the other is not.' The Tests were so bad tempered and fraught and Australians so angry that the series almost became a serious diplomatic incident. To Australians as a whole, the upper-class, supercilious English captain reminded them of class-ridden England and its continuing condescension towards the colonists. Many Australians of that generation would never forget the Bodyline series and memories of it became a spur to beat the Poms for some decades.

Australian politicans have also understood that the Test team is a tangible example of our identity and know it's good politics to bask in its reflected glory. A look at a list of Australian politicians who have done so is instructive. It begins from the very first Prime Minister, Edmond Barton, who umpired in the notorious riot-interrupted Test of 1879. The great Alfred Deakin loved the game. Menzies once said that, 'If I ever reach Valhalla I hope to find cricketers seated on my left and right, because I feel happy in their company.' Pipe-smoking former train driver Ben Chifley said of cricket that it 'produces a million things of beauty for the eye'. Legman Harold Holt was once a reasonable leg spin bowler. Bob Hawke was a rather proficient player although one of the most famous news photographs of him is of him reeling away as a bouncer shatters his spectacles. John Howard, who once cravenly faced his own people dressed in a bulletproof jacket, calls himself a 'cricket tragic'. Probably it is writer Tom Keneally who best summed up what the politicians see in the game: 'We may be a small and callow race but there is divinity in our cricket.'

The only other consistent symbol of our national identity is the spirit of Gallipoli and it is fascinating how

Waugh's team co-opted it so that the two, sport and war, seemed to be one and the same. Prior to the 2001 tour of England, the Australian team visited Gallipoli and re-enacted for the cameras the famous photograph of Australian troops playing cricket on the beaches of Anzac Cove. They had used the match as a distraction for the Turks while Australian troops were quietly smuggled onto ships to slip away after losing the gruesome, long battle. Some commentators were appalled by Waugh's action but it was difficult to believe that those ghosts who still haunt Gallipoli wouldn't have understood the gesture. After all, many of those dead men would have gone straight from the cricket fields into the army to fight on foreign soil.

For most of the team the visit was extremely moving and Waugh asked his players for their reactions. For Glenn McGrath, your archetypal Aussie country boy, it gave him an understanding as to why we march on Anzac Day, but also niggling questions about why we were fighting the Turks and why did we land on the wrong spot? Others felt proud and emotional. A tremendously moved Adam Gilchrist was articulate as usual and, like many of his team-mates, found himself drawing parallels between sport and war. 'We certainly felt emotions akin to this at the end of the recent Indian Test series that we lost narrowly. Of course the stakes were obviously much higher in World War I and in any war for that matter, than in a simple game of cricket. How sad, almost ironic it is that we can draw motivation from the deaths of our heroes who never returned.' Warne's reflections were elliptic: 'Sacrifice of people …

commitment.' For Steve Waugh the visit was highly emotional because he saw Gallipoli, as do many Australians, as a place where our national identity was formed. He told reporters that future teams should visit Anzac Cove because he saw it as a sacred place for cricketers to renew their sense of tradition.

This conflation of Gallipoli and cricket is reflected elsewhere, including in books and films. In the Australian film *Break of Day* (1976) the hero is a man who shot himself in the foot at Gallipoli in order to be shipped out. After the war he is regarded as a coward by some of the townspeople where he lives. The seminal scene of the movie revolves around a game of cricket where the limping Tom attempts to bat his team to victory, but the opposing fast bowler bowls him vicious bouncer after bouncer until Tom is hit, the result of which is a wild brawl. In this game of cricket Tom has had to fight the battle of Gallipoli again, only this time he proves himself a real man; just as our troops were defeated but proved themselves to be brave, so, given a second chance, Tom, although defeated, proves himself by bravely facing up to the bouncers.

It's interesting that in portraying a national sport, movies can reflect a vivid sense of national identity. In the United States baseball is more than a game; it is a metaphor for the American dream and through such films as *Fear Strikes Out* (1957), *The Natural* (1984), *Bull Durham* (1988), *Field of Dreams* (1989) and *Cobb* (1994) one can see the dream flourish or sour. For Americans baseball is tradition and a chance for reflection on its basic belief in the crucial importance of the individual in its society.

In the same way English films about cricket reflect something about the nation. In films like *The Final Test* (1953), *Accident* (1967), *The Go-Between* (1971) and *Another Country* (1984) one sees through the game of cricket the permanence of the class system, a sense that the tradition of cricket is a ritual of people knowing their place, and the symbolic undertow of the game as a living cocoon of a lost Eden. Other films use cricket as a way of undercutting such uncertainties. In *The Shout* (1978) mental patients and cricketers symbolically collide as if reflecting the chaotic self-image of England at the time. In *Playing Away* (1990) the contest between black and white teams is a serious reflection of the racial conflicts in contemporary English society. Even in *The Crying Game* (1992) cricket has a metaphorical resonance, as a game that hides an unnatural, even perverse heart under its traditional exterior.

The Australian mini-series *Bodyline* carried huge metaphorical and symbolic issues, especially in the relationship between England, the Mother Country, and Australia, its colonial outpost. The series reinforced the theme that England was a soulless cricketing machine and, although it regards itself as the home of cricketing traditions, it is actually the Australians who are upholding those traditions of sportsmanship. In the film *Burke and Wills* (1986) cricket is used as a symbol of misunderstanding between Aborigines and whites. A tribe of Aborigines accidentally comes upon the eponymous explorers playing a game of cricket at Cooper Creek. Their bewilderment at this strange game extends to daft

Wills explaining to the uncomprehending Aborigines, 'This is a cricket bat. Hit the ball.'

The irony, of course, is that the 1868 Aboriginal team was the first Australian cricket team to tour England. Since then no full-blooded Aborigines have played for Australia, though current Test player Jason Gillespie is part-Aboriginal, and even now the present team does not reflect the multicultural make-up of our society. In recent years the English team has been called 'The Commonwealth Eleven'. The players' countries of origin have ranged widely. Andy Caddick was born in New Zealand, Nasser Hussain, the present captain, was born in Madras. Robin Smith and Allan Lamb were born in South Africa. Zimbabwe produced Phil Edmonds, Graeme Hick and Neal Radford. Derek Pringle was born in Nairobi. The West Indies supplied Norman Cowans, Phil DeFreitas, Chris Lewis, Devon Malcolm and Gladstone Small. Hong Kong even chimed in by providing the English with Dermot Reeve. This is not to say that there weren't criticisms of such a 'Foreign Legion'. One English cricket writer was howled down when he suggested that England's recent dismal record in Test cricket could be explained by the fact that many of the cricketers, because of their scattered birthplaces, were playing for themselves and not England. The mixture of blacks and whites in the team certainly didn't mean that the English team and staff were now one hundred per cent politically correct. During the 1995–96 tour of South Africa the English cricket manager, former Test captain Ray Illingworth, was alleged to have called the black English bowler Devon Malcolm a 'nig-nog'.

Although the Indian team is predominantly Hindu, Muslims like Muhammad Azharuddin can rise to become captain. In contemporary South Africa the national team is undergoing a transformation as the Cricket Board insists on at least two 'coloured' players being in the Test team, a piece of affirmative action that was to cause unrest in the South Africa team when it was touring Australia in 2001–02. For the Third and final Test of the series United Cricket Board of South Africa president Percy Sonn vetoed the team management's selection choice and forced them to choose coloured cricketer Justin Ontong in place of the white Jacques Rudolph. Even though he batted well in the Test the public knew Ontong was chosen for more than his merit.

By contrast Australian Test cricketers are basically an Anglo-Celtic bunch, something that irritates many commentators who find it appalling that the team doesn't reflect the multicultural mix of contemporary Australian society. Writing in the *Sydney Morning Herald*, during the 1998–99 Ashes tour, journalist Pilita Clark was even aghast at the racial make-up of the spectators: 'Consider the average SCG crowd. We are not talking United Nations here.' From the crowd it was an easy segue to the ethnic make-up of the Australian team: 'Worse, look at the Test team itself. Other mass-appeal sports, such as Aussie Rules football, rugby or even tennis … have managed to diversify. Aborigines and people from non-English-speaking backgrounds have played at the highest levels of these sports for years, unconsciously sending a message of inclusion and unity to millions.' To the columnist Clark, whose lack of humour is her trade-mark, the added insult is that because the media spotlight is so heavily focused on cricket it furnishes a distorted picture of our nation and its culture: 'Here we still have a bunch of overwhelmingly Anglo-Celtic boys from the suburbs who, together, look nothing like today's Australia. And yet summer after summer, year after year, the news media treat them as if they are not merely representatives of the culture, but cultural repre-sentatives.'

Clark is quite right, of course, about the complexion of both the crowd and our contemporary teams. Aus-tralian crowds can be racist. In the 1990s the West Indian fast bowler, Patrick Patterson, when fielding near the boundary in Perth, had to put up with sections of the crowd yelling 'Woof, woof! Throw him a banana!'. Even recently Australian supporters in Calcutta con-stantly abused the Indians, yelling out, 'Get fucked you curry-munching bastards!' But it should be pointed out that there have been cricketers of Yugoslav (Lenny Pascoe-Durtanovich), Italian (Michael Veletta) and Tongan/ New Zealand (Brendon Julian) background who have played for Australia. There has also been a Chinese-Australian, Richard Chee Quee, who played for New South Wales. Yet these are exceptions and the situation perplexes Australian cricket authorities, who are keen to widen the appeal of the game.

The desire to have a much wider spectrum of ethnic players at Test level is well-intentioned and necessary for the health of the game, but there are obstacles. One-day games may have a superficial excitement but any boy knows that the ultimate aim of any cricketer is to play Test cricket, a game that goes on for five days. For many ethnic youths this is not an attractive notion, especially in an era where the American influence is so powerful and insidious. Basketball is of short duration and is a fast, high-scoring game, that comes with the glamorous aura of its American-ness. Many youths probably know the names of American basketballers but couldn't name an Australian cricketer. For newly arrived immigrant families, study comes first and sport is regarded as frivolous. Other ethnic groups are certainly not sports-mad. For instance, it is almost impossible to think of a Jewish cricketer who has played Test cricket for any country – apart from the Australian Test opener Julian Wiener. And lastly, even though Australia plays teams from the subcontinent, the dominant Test series is against England, which makes little sense at all, given that the recent English sides have been so substandard. But it does make sense historically. England is 'the home' of cricket and Australian teams always want to win the Ashes, almost as a matter of national pride. For ethnic youths, this historical connection does not hold much attraction, just as the powerful historical resonance of Gallipoli means little. Former captain Allan Border is right when he writes: 'Patriotism, nationalism, love of country – call it what you will – certainly isn't fashionable nowadays. Nor is the idea that team players should always play for the team first, not for themselves.' Fashionable or not, it is obvious that both values counted heavily with Waugh's men. It's what motivated them to win match after match, sometimes from unwinnable positions.

Witness the reverence the players have for the baggy green cap. Or witness their willingness to burst into the team song 'Under The Southern Cross I Stand' after a victory. The Prime Minister, John Howard, recognised this: 'The team members take pride in the tradition of playing for their country and in their loyalty to one another.' This attitude is something that is not immediately appealing to ethnic kids, especially when it is tied up with a slightly jingoistic nationalism, as illustrated in the lyrics of the team song which go: 'Under the Southern Cross I stand/A sprig of wattle in my hand/A native of my native land/Australia, you bloody beauty.' (Although the tired and emotional version after a great victory goes: 'Two hands, two steely cans/under the Southern Cross we stand/A sprig of wattle in our hands/a tribute to our native land/Australia you fucking beauty/Up the jolly red rooster and drink more piss!')

Waugh's team is a traditional mixture of country boys, the working class, and some from the middle class and it emphasises the strength of classlessness and it is no accident that except for Warne none of the present players have attended private schools. This is a team that celebrates old-fashioned virtues like mateship and the highest praise that someone can bestow on another is to call him, in Ian Healy's words, 'a dead set mate'. The team is strongly heterosexual and despises the glamour of celebrating individual success that attaches itself to soccer, rugby or Australian Rules players. It is the team that comes first and in its essence it is a defiant example of the national characteristic of The Tall Poppy

Syndrome, the cutting down of those who 'get too big for their boots'.

In his book *We're Right Behind You, Captain!*, the English writer David Hopps attempts to sum up what is different about the Australian cricket culture compared to the English team: 'There is little doubt that the Australian team feels a more powerful sense of national identity than its English counterpart. That is not the fault of the England players, but the system in which they have been raised. The essence of that Australian pride is summed up in the concept of "mateship". No other single word sums up Australia's image of itself. It might be difficult for the English to define but the laconic, easygoing, outspoken, uncomplicated and sociable qualities of the country are all part of it. Its intention is to unite all ages, all backgrounds. In its simplest form, it is a basic expression of community.'

It is precisely these qualities that made Waugh's team such a fabulous success. Commentators may bemoan the fact but this is a team that is unified by its common attributes of Anglo-Celtic background, class and culture. It reflects an era seemingly long past, a country that had a united culture, values and a single identity. Waugh has heard the faint echoes of these values and beliefs and amplified them to make them a major reason behind the team's success. He has seen other cricketing nations undermined by ethnic and cultural and religious differences – and even in the case of the West Indians, island allegiances interfering with the national team selections – and decided that it is not old-fashioned to talk of national pride. That is why he has transformed the baggy green cap into such a fetishistic symbol of what it means to be an Australian cricketer. On the morning of the first day of fielding in a Test all members of the team wear it and are inordinately proud to do so.

Australia has always played the game hard. Back in 1950 the English cricket commentator John Arlott said of the Australian cricket philosophy that it involved 'a single-minded determination to win the game – to win within laws, but if necessary to the last limit within them.' This approach and this vigorous national pride have come with other not-so-attractive features, especially the brutal art of sledging, of which Australians have become masters. There has always been on-field abuse of an opponent to put him off his game. However, it was in the 1970s that the teams that Ian Chappell led started to openly verbally harass opposition players. It was a part of Chappell's win-at-all-costs mentality. Simultaneously intelligent, gruff and boorish, Chappell wanted to psychologically destroy opponents. Dennis Lillee was a fearsome practitioner of sledging. The English batsman Bob Woolmer had to put up with Lillee's relentless abuse during one long innings, in which Woolmer said he became fully aquainted with the Australian alphabet: 'It started with f and ended with f.' As far as Chappell is concerned the term 'sledging' had its origin at a party in the mid-1960s where the fast bowler Grahame Corling swore in front of a waitress. A team-mate rebuked him, saying he was as subtle as a sledgehammer. Corling's nickname then became 'Percy' after the singer Percy Sledge (who had a hit record of the time, 'When a Man Loves a Woman'). After that any cricketer who made a *faux pas* in front of a woman was called a 'sledge' or accused of 'sledging'.

Warne was introduced to one of the masters of sledging, Merv Hughes, who was a flagrant and compulsive sledger. From outside the boundary fence it was hard to take the bushy-mustachioed fast bowler, with the beer belly that swung in counter-rhythm to the rest of his body when he came into bowl, as anything more than a cartoon bully. But on the field he could be intimidating and his constant sledging was effective. A Sheffield Shield opponent, James Brayshaw, remembers Hughes abusing him after the first ball he faced: 'It was the most personal vitriol I have ever, ever received: "You faggot, you cocksucker, you dirty little prick".' To the English captain Nasser Hussain sledging was the definitive difference between the cricketing cultures: 'The Aussies even in their grade cricket are abusing you and rucking you. Our club cricket, in comparison, is like a social gathering.'

By the early 1990s the Australian team was earning the reputation as the 'Ugly Australians'. Their sledging was blatant and obnoxiously crude and the authorities became increasingly concerned about Australia's image. After Hughes was fined for his verbal abuse in South Africa during the 1995 tour, English opener Michael Atherton was amazed at his transformation. Hughes didn't say a word to him: 'I had to ask him whether he couldn't pay his fine and the ACB had taken his tonsils out as punishment.' It was up to Mark Taylor to try to limit the amount of sledging but Taylor, always reluctant to enforce discipline, allowed it to thrive, albeit in a more subtle form. For someone like the seemingly meek medium-fast bowler Paul Reiffel, there was a distinction between gamesmanship and sledging: 'Gamesmanship is more subtle … Ian Healy is brilliant at it. He might say something that is totally irrelevant to the game, or to anything, really. He won't have sworn; he won't even have raised his voice. It's just chatter. But if it causes the batsman to stop and think about what Heals has said, it might distract him just long enough to make him give his wicket away. If that's sledging, I think it's good sledging.' When Waugh took over the Australian team his severity and aggression were reinforced by concentrated sledging that frequently burst into pure verbal venom that was even more personal. He also continued the ugly policy of bowlers celebrating wildly in the batsman's face when he was out, even at times following him off the pitch. Other teams sledged but not to the extent of the Australians. The English decided to mimic the Australians in order to toughen their approach to Test matches. In the middle–1990s the English went after the intense Michael Bevan, relentlessly sledging him with what were said to be words overheard coming from Bevan's hotel room one night. Whatever the Australian uttered in that room worked for the English, because he had a poor series.

As far as Steve Waugh is concerned, sledging is a way of gaining a psychological edge over his opponents. Like Reiffel, Waugh also likes to distinguish between gamesmanship and sledging and places it all under the one rubric: 'the policy of mental disintegration'. Waugh is being a trifle disingenuous here. The fact is that his

team is notorious for sledging. In preparation for their
tour of Australia in 2001–02 the South Africans sought
the advice of former Test off spinner and 'chief motor-
mouth' Pat Symcox to help deal with Australian
sledging. He said the team should focus on opening
batsman, Matt Hayden, who had failed so badly against
them a few years before that he was dropped. They were
instructed to say to Hayden: 'I'd shut up if I was you.
The last time you played us it cost you three years of
your career.' But it didn't work. Hayden had such a
successful trio of Tests that he was named man-of-the-
series. Justin Ontong, a controversial selection for his
début Test match, because it was seen as an example of
affirmative action, batted fluently in his first Test and was
sledged relentlessly. 'I would just like to say they got very
personal sometimes,' he said after the match, acknowl-
edging that the South Africans had been worn down by
the constant barbs. As far as Ontong was concerned the
Australian sledging plus their mental strength and sense
of purpose all combined to mentally crush the South
African team. After Australia toured South Africa in
2002 the young South African batsman Graeme Smith
was horrified at the way he was sledged during his début
Test. He singled out certain players as the main offend-
ers and said that when he went out to bat Hayden, a
fervent Christian who crosses himself after he scores a
century, followed him to the crease and stood 'right in
my face' for about two minutes, abusing him: 'You
know, you're not fucking good enough. How the fuck
are you going to handle Shane Warne when he's bowling in the rough?' Warne spent the whole day calling the

South African a cunt or varying it with 'you fucking cunt, what are you doing here!' And, just as other batsmen have discovered when having to deal with Australian sledging, Smith found himself engaged in 'a big battle to stay calm'.

For the past few years, except for a hiccup in India in 2001 where the home side won one of the most exciting Test series for many years, Australia has been incredibly successful. Waugh's team is universally respected and admired but their harsh mental tactics and chauvinistic sense of identity are interpreted by some countries as insolence and arrogance. And indeed the Australian team reflects the pride Australians feel in their cohesive, peaceful society. The subcontinent, the West Indies and South Africa are seen as places of violence, social unrest and bewildering faiths and ethnic tensions. When he was asked if he had any regrets about boycotting a one-day game at Colombo in the 1996 World Cup because of the threat of terrorism, Australian captain Mark Taylor tried to explain the cultural differences: 'People tell us when we're here that we have to understand other people's cultures and we try hard to do that. But I'd like people to look at things from both sides. Put yourselves in our shoes and look at the way we live in Australia compared to the way other people live in the subcontinent.' His comments upset his subcontinental hosts who took it as a not-too-subtle hint that their part of the world was prone to constant violence and terrorism. During Warne's career he has seen matches cancelled in Sri Lanka because of terrorism, players having to flee crowd riots in the West Indies, tours of Pakistan cancelled or changed to another venue because of political unrest, war and terrorist bombings and a tour of Zimbabwe cancelled because of the syphilitic madman and despot Mugabe. By comparison, the biggest problems Australian cricket authorities have to deal with are streakers and unruly drunken crowds at one-day games. Overseas tours have convinced Australian cricketers that their society is indeed 'the lucky country'.

Warne has found in the Australian team's unabashed chauvinism a sense of community and an ethos of what it means to be Australian. It may be old-fashioned to some but to him and his team-mates it is both a powerful bond and a successful formula for winning. Warne has flourished in this environment of national pride and he has used the strong bond between the players and the team's profoundly personal concept of mateship to psychologically protect him when it seemed that the world outside the dressing-room and off the field was out to get him.

12: Apotheosis

By the time Warne was picked to tour South Africa in early 2002, he had played nearly one hundred Test matches. Again he had struggled in India during the 2001 series and was devastated when the new coach, John Buchanan, caused headlines with public comments about his fitness and hinted that Warne may have a limited future in the team. His ego was considerably bruised. As Waugh said, defending his celebrated spinner: 'Statements made about superstars such as Warney have a completely different impact from a rev-up of a player in domestic cricket.'

Later in the same year Warne, as usual, bowled superbly against the English in England and took 31 wickets for a measly 18 runs per wicket. But as Bob Simpson had remarked, with tongue half in his cheek, Australian selectors no longer paid attention to a player's form against the old adversary. The nation to beat in order to become the number one team was South Africa. In 2001 and 2002 there were to be two Test series between the nations. The first three-match series would be played in Australia and the return series in South Africa. It was thought that this was going to be closely fought and it would be no surprise if South Africa won. But Waugh confidently predicted that Australia would win the series 6-nil.

Despite his success in England, something that the public fully expected against the weak English, Warne's Test series against New Zealand in Australia was mediocre to say the least. In the three rain-affected Tests he took only six wickets at an average of over 70 runs. It was the third-worst result of his career. Although he had a very good record against the South Africans there were rumblings that he was past his prime, and much to his chagrin there were calls for Stuart MacGill to replace him. The old bluster was there, however, and he used the media to let the South Africans know that his ability to bowl the flipper had returned. But he was worried. He brought in his mentor, Terry Jenner, to try to mend the flaws that were becoming obvious in his bowling, but tried to underplay this by saying it was merely his 10,000-ball overhaul and tune-up. Whatever it was, Warne bowled beautifully in the First Test, taking 8-170 for the match and winning the man-of-the-match award (and who could keep count of how many he has won over the years?). But it was more than his match figures that impressed. His flipper may have been reasonable rather than dangerous but his leg breaks had that delightful loop and drift towards leg stump before the sharp turn and bounce to off that characterises his best bowling and which causes batsmen to give many an inside edge catch to close-in fielders. His accuracy had returned and he attacked the leg stump, which invades the batsman's territory, sometimes called 'the blind spot'.

Australia won the three-Test series and Warne bowled excellently. In the final Test in Sydney he bowled in tandem with Stuart MacGill and, even though he was bowling with a man who makes him uneasy because he is competition, it was the best they had bowled together. Watching the game, with the faint smell of the devastating NSW bushfires still drifting in the air, it was instructive to see the differences between the two leg spinners, especially on the last day when Kirsten stubbornly refused to give away his wicket. MacGill's run-up was quick and direct and he spun the ball with a flatter trajectory but his bounce and turn were prodigious. By contrast Warne's run-up seemed more a casual walk. Unlike MacGill he quickly settled into a familiar and predictable rhythm, as if he were lulling the batsmen into complacency and then waiting for them to make a mistake. MacGill had an intensity, an anger about him that occasionally upset his own rhythm. Although bowling steadily, Warne seemed anxious, as if he were trying to summon up inner mental strengths that were waning. There seemed to be a sense that he didn't quite believe he could make the breakthroughs, and when they came they seemed more a relief than a jubilant justification of the way he was bowling. MacGill made the batsmen play quickly and uncertainly and it seemed that he was always going to take a wicket even if he did throw up the occasional bad ball. Gradually the two men wore down the South African resistance and it was MacGill who finally took the patient Kirsten's wicket by bowling him. At the end he had four wickets and Warne three. For Warne the danger signs were there and he would have sensed the truth of cricket journalist Mike Coward's words: 'It was MacGill rather than Warne who turned heads yesterday with his prodigious turn and superior control.'

If that weren't enough Warne's bowling in the one-day series was shoddy. He seemed lethargic and reluctant to impart much spin on the ball, as if he had allocated for himself the curious role of a containing bowler, which was at odds with his talent and personality. The result was headlines and stories that called him the worst bowler of the series, with the worst strike rate and the worst average. There was increasing media speculation that it was only a matter of time before MacGill replaced him in the one-day side.

Yet Warne had reason to be hopeful that he still had a future in one-day cricket. Earlier in the season he had been made vice-captain of the Australian one-day team against New Zealand when Gilchrist was absent. When Steve Waugh was dropped as captain of the one-day team Warne was entitled to feel optimistic that he was up for the job. He knew he had great support within the selection panel and his temporary role as vice-captain seemed to imply that the majority of Board members had pardoned him for the telephone sex scandal. But he still had his critics. No longer the golden boy, he was tainted and stained by his own antics. One letter writer in the *Sydney Morning Herald* summed up the typical anti-Warne sentiment: 'Shane Warne's return to the vice-captaincy may be part of a creative ACB strategy to neutralise the MCG yobs by promoting one of their own.'

When Ricky Ponting was made captain and Gilchrist vice-captain of the one-day team before the start of the 2002 Test series in South Africa Warne was devastated and criticised the selectors for giving him 'mixed messages'. Quite rightly he said that they had unfairly raised his hopes: 'When I was appointed vice-captain this year … I thought my chances [for future captaincy] were pretty good.' Preparing for the First Test match in Johannesburg he felt crushed and realised that his dream of being captain was gone forever. There were even signs that the media and selectors had lost faith in his ability in the short version of the game. He had played 175 one-day games and wondered aloud if he could still be a major contributor to the form: 'I'd like to think so, but you don't know what is down the track,' said a dispirited Warne. 'It is not up to us to pick the side. I think I still have a lot to offer the one-day team. Whether the selectors think that is up to them.' It was a vintage Warne performance. A mixture of childish petulance, a general moan and an impotent flailing against perceived injustice. Long-term team-mates had become used to Warne's mood swings. In the privacy of the dressing-room he could be ebullient and boyishly happy, but when the outside world attacked or threatened him he retreated into moping and occasional bitterness. You couldn't call it melancholia because that presupposes deep introspection. These moods are not so reflective, but more a plaintive moan of *Why me*? And if in his glumness and general railings against the world he needed reminding that he could easily be replaced, he need only look across the dressing-room and see MacGill, also chosen for the tour, waiting to partner him or supplant him. And if that wasn't enough to distract him, there were also the headlines about the attempted extortion case involving teenage girls and their uncle that had been in all the newspapers just after his arrival in South Africa.

He had been playing Test cricket for a decade and the various injuries, mistimed comebacks, controversies and selection decisions would have worn down another man, but, as is his character, he refused to simply make a graceful exit or even allow others to dictate to him that he was finished. His ultra-competitiveness and single-minded concentration surfaced. As did his pride. Never forget his pride. In speaking to the press he may understate his contribution to Australian cricket and his own prowess, but in private he values both greatly. To not understand how proud he is of his career is to misunderstand his character.

In the lead-up game to the Test series Adam Gilchrist, a man whose simple and unaffected manner hides a rich emotional complexity, noticed Warne leaving the distractions off the field and he talked of how the spinner's mystique enveloped the South Africans and even now, after playing with Warne for many Tests, he spoke openly of how he still felt a shiver down his spine when keeping to him. It seemed to Gilchrist and his team-mates that Warne was psyching himself up to perform well. And it was not only that, he looked different and younger. Knowing his natural talent had to be helped along as he aged, Warne had embarked on a diet in order to prolong his career. He gave up his lurid diet of pizza, cheese sandwiches, potato chips, sausage rolls and vanilla slices. Perversely, he didn't replace his favourite foods with anything else. He merely ate cereal and baked beans and gave up beer for water. He lost eight kilograms in two months and hadn't looked as fit and slim for over ten years.

Ever since his days at the Cricket Academy, his diet had been atrocious for a sportsman. Although mocked for his roly-poly shape after his disastrous début, he still hadn't stopped eating and even during his second Test had midnight feasts of junk food with his fellow Victorian, Merv Hughes. Hughes himself could have prolonged his career if he had lost weight but was unable to stop bingeing. The astute Australian physiotherapist Errol Alcott once theorised that Hughes ate so much because he was still fighting his inner doubts whether he belonged at Test level. Warne's weight oscillated wildly for a decade. Mostly he was plump or fat, mostly he pretended he wasn't bothered by the abuse that centred on his weight, mostly he pretended to enjoy the stories about his weird diet. Team-mates told anecdotes about him going to a Japanese restaurant only to ask the waitress to go next door and get him a pizza. There were the mocking headlines about his dislike of Indian food when, after pining for cans of baked beans during a tour of India, Heinz sent him nearly two thousand cans. For all his bravado that he didn't care what people said, the relentless focus on his weight and constant mocking niggled him and on one memorable occasion in 1997 at a photo opportunity that had him unveil a wax replica of himself for Madame Tussaud's, a reporter asked him how his weight compared to that of the slimmer wax dummy. An upset Warne stormed out of the room, leaving behind amused reporters and the promise of headlines and mocking stories for the next morning's papers.

Now that he was slimmer and fitter and determined to extend his career, he had to prove he was still an intimidating presence on the field. In the First Test he took six wickets and in so doing became the second-highest wicket taker in Test cricket. He had taken 436 wickets in 99 matches, and was closing the gap on Courtney Walsh who took 519 wickets in his 132-game career. But it was in his next and hundredth Test that Warne produced one of his greatest achievements, an effort that reinforced or reminded people of his singular skill and mental toughness.

Playing this Test was a special milestone for him. After playing in his first Test he thought it was the only one he would ever play. Even in his wildest fantasies he probably never believed he would play one hundred. He was also desperately keen for Australia to win because it would mean they would take an unbeatable lead in the three-match series. And if Australia won and he bowled well it would make the Test even more of a special occasion. He knew that his critics, of which there were many, were questioning his longevity in the game. Many could point to his statistics since his shoulder operation. Before he had surgery he was averaging 24 runs per wicket, now it was nearly 32. You could see that after each operation he trusted his body less and a graph would show that the speed of his deliveries kept escalating as he found himself not trusting his slower deliveries, even though they had once turned more. Quite simply, he couldn't spin the ball as far as he used to. But what he had lost in natural ability he had gained in wisdom. As he said, preparing for this special game: 'When I first started I didn't understand the what, the when and why of bowling. I just rocked up and bowled big leg breaks and they might nick one and get out and everyone would say I bowled well because I beat the bat a lot. Now I'm a bit more cagey and more experienced. I work the batsmen out better than I used to.' He knew no bowler had ever taken five wickets in his 100th Test match but he went into the Test with what can only be labelled the determination of a champion. If anyone was to win the game, it was going to be him.

South Africa scored 239 in the first innings, Australia scored 382, but in the second innings the pitch had dried out and the fast bowlers found the hot conditions and unresponsive wicket trying. Warne had scored 63 in the first innings to become only the fourth player to take 400 wickets and make 2000 runs, and now set out to single-handedly contain the South Africans and also to take wickets on a perfect batting pitch. He knew after the first few overs that it would not be easy. It wasn't like the First Test where the conditions suited Warne, here in Cape Town he would have to be even more cunning and shrewd. Each wicket would be difficult to earn. By the time he came on to bowl it was obvious that none of the other bowlers were going to make consistent breakthroughs. It looked like it would be a heartbreaking and arduous day.

I was temporarily out of my Kings Cross apartment and renting a hotel room in a daggy 1970s motel/hotel in Potts Point that overlooked Garden Island where several naval ships were docked, their engines humming and throbbing gently through the night. My own neighbourhood was changing. Kings Cross was and is in the process of being gentrified and the noise of drills, sledgehammers, cranes, and other noisy machines was proving intolerable. I was writing this book and needed somewhere quieter. I shifted into the hotel because it had cable TV. The commercial television channels weren't showing the cricket and at least I could watch the South African matches, hoping they would be as thrilling as the Test series in India, which commercial television also refused to show. Watching Warne bowl his opening spell in his hundreth Test, I had an acute sense of *déjà vu*. In his early overs he seemed to be bowling as in Sydney. His bowling seemed to lack penetration. What I mean is that unlike earlier in his career, when every ball seemed to threaten and promise surprise and variation, he had quickly settled into a rhythm of line and length. There was no outrageous spin and even when he hit the footmarks there was not enough roughage to cause the ball to deviate to a great degree. But as I sat there I was mesmerised, because what he was doing was illustrating the difference between an immature and stunningly original bowler and a mature bowler who was slowly but surely wearing down the batsmen with impeccable and nagging length, control and subtle variations of flight and a cunning and yet sparse demonstration of the various deliveries he could bowl. It was a war of attrition and he was going to prove he had the greater skill and the better concentration.

He was to bowl the most overs he had bowled in a Test match day (42), in an innings (70) and concede the most runs (161) in an innings, but in doing so he took six wickets when all of the other bowlers could only take two wickets in five sessions. This was a marathon and inspiring effort of profound concentration, skill, guile, deception and craft. Through the long hot day Warne refused to stop bowling. He was convinced that only he had the ability to take the wickets and rein in the scoring. At times it seemed like Warne versus South Africa. His saturnine intensity, his unbreakable spirit was breathtaking. Here was a man who had been told he was washed-up many a time recently. Here was a champion who was thought to be past match-winning deeds. Countless times he had read his cricket obituaries, but he just wouldn't give up. Most of the batsmen got good starts but inexorably Warne took one wicket and then another one. There was no sudden fall of wickets, only a game of patience as the South African batsmen, many of whom should have gone on to score centuries, finally mentally stumbled and played a loose or tentative shot. Later he was to sardonically refer to the effort: 'When I hit the 60-over mark it was like a big night out – you get your third and fourth wind. It gets past midnight and when you get to two o'clock you get that third wind.' In reality he knew he had done something special. His marathon spell was a personal vindication. He proved to Buchanan that he could bowl long spells in oppressive conditions, he reminded his fellow players that he was crucial to the team and he reminded the South Africans that they should never take him for granted, not that they ever had, but this was a pitch where they could have taken to him if he had bowled badly. Above all he took immense pride in the fact that it was his hundredth Test and he wasn't going to even consider defeat. It was an epic illustration of the leg spinner's craft and perhaps one of his most remarkable performances. At the end of the day he had taken four wickets. Next day he came back to resume the battle. Exhausted, enervated and with aching muscles, he set about taking the remaining wickets. Over the years the various parts of his right arm, its hand and fingers and its shoulder, their muscles, bones, cartilage and tendons had been torn, worn and broken. Surgeons had cut tissue, muscles and rearranged bones in order to repair him. Really, he should have given up and retired some years before, but his willpower and his desire to prove himself once again prevailed and he won – he took two more wickets. It was a supreme victory of mind over body. He helped restrict South Africa's lead to 330. In a tense finish Warne joined Ponting after the fall of another quick wicket and, again determined to win, he slashed a four through slips and then stroked two more fours to help Australia win by four wickets. If any game summed up Warne's extraordinary talent, his unwillingness to give in and his personal pride then this was the Test. No-one now could question his right to be called a champion.

At the end of the game as he walked around the ground accepting the plaudits of the crowd with his team-mates, who were celebrating their victory in the series and confirming themselves as the number one cricket team in the world, Warne paused and smiled on spotting his wife and children. It was a smile of relief. He had come through again and confounded all doubters, mealy-mouthed critics and the selectors. For the exhausted spinner this was a sublime moment. Despite all the controversies, scandals and mistakes, he had proved himself once again in the only place where off-field distractions vanished and where he could realise, against all odds, his special genius.

13: Shane's World

Warne has achieved more success than he ever dreamt he would. He is the most famous cricketer since Bradman. He is one of the great bowlers of all time. He is celebrated and a celebrity. He has earned millions from his special prowess. He is both loved and reviled. He has written, well at least dictated, his autobiography at the age of 32. Just as he made sure that every time he bowled there was a heightened expectation that wickets would fall, so the journey of his short life has been lived at a heightened pace and most of it in the public gaze.

For a time there was a fad in screenplay writing. It was thought the key to a successful film was the universal and mythic concept of the hero's Journey. Based on Joseph Campbell's popularisation of common strands of certain myths and legends from across the world, the theory was that for a story to be successful and appeal to everyone it had to be underpinned by the journey of the central character or the hero. In its basic form the hero sets out on a quest and before he reaches the end he has to undergo many trials and tribulations. The beginning of his journey is more of a stumble than a confident step forward and he will need the help of mentors to go further. He will prove himself brave and vanquish obstacles put in his way and overcome his own deficiencies of character. He will sometimes momentarily retreat, but his journey is always forward. He will symbolically die and be reborn and will carry the aspirations of his tribe or people. He will confront enemies and some friends will turn out to be enemies. At the end of his journey he will either die fulfilling his quest or return with the prize or elixir, call it what you will. In a way Warne's 'journey' has a similar structure. Because of his specific genius he is a hero to many but along the way he has had to overcome his own demons as a cricketer, including the injuries and the jackals of the press. He has carried the aspirations of Australians every time he has played Test cricket. He has fallen by the wayside when his own character deficiencies have tripped him up. Every step of the way has been taken in the public gaze, so every success, every fault or flaw has been magnified. And just when it was thought he was washed-up or had stumbled in his quest, there was an effort like his marathon spell in South Africa in 2002. It is because he fulfils certain innate and mythic aspects of the hero's journey that he intrigues so many millions.

Of course I'm not saying that he is a hero. He has done many heroic things on the cricket paddock, but he is not a warrior or a man who has saved lives. It was a true hero, Keith Miller, a fighter pilot in World War II, who concisely put cricket into a larger context when he said: 'I guess you don't get carried away when you've known what it is like to have a Messerschmitt up your arse.' Cricket is not life, but it is a part of it. The English cricketer Colin Cowdrey once wondered aloud if he could justify having spent a quarter of a century batting or standing at first slip. Ian Woolridge, cricket writer, said of Cowdrey's regret: 'As understatements go, that probably ranks with [the celebrated violinist] Menuhin dismissing his life as one long fiddle.' It is a game that can seem strangely pointless in the modern era. To play a game for five days and be satisfied with a lack of a result is to defy commonsense and seems closer to the tediously slow unfolding of a ten-hour Noh drama than an action movie. Groucho Marx once attended a game at Lord's and after watching it for an hour asked if the game had started yet. For the ignorant it seems undramatic but for the *aficionado* it has mini-drama within mini-drama, not unlike the French writer Raymond Roussel's poems and prose which don't seem to move forward because of his technique of parenthesis within parenthesis within parenthesis. It is a game that is defiantly backward-looking and nostalgic. For a full appreciation of it, especially from a spectator's viewpoint, it is important to see the importance of a particular feat in its historic context, hence the fetishistic attachment to statistics that bewilders the uninitiated.

And the game is more than a game. For all those nations that play at Test level, the way the game is played, the way a nation has incorporated its particular values into a sport that was invented by the English and only

spread across the globe as an adjunct to its imperial conquests, the way certain players, Bradman, Botham, Warne
and Tendulkar, have carried the hopes of their nation
when they play it (the many suicides of fans in the subcontinent after their teams have lost testifies to its
importance) and the way it is reflected in art and popular culture shows its power and continuing potency.
This is a sport that seems a team game but which is
really a lonely game, where the individual has to constantly confront his own inner strengths and weaknesses.

But the significant and symbolic place of cricket in a
nation's consciousness is due to men who are merely
playing. Cricket is literally a game and Warne happens to
be particularly brilliant at it. He is no intellectual, nor
does he have a great grasp of its history. He has no interest in reading or high culture. He is not as thick as the
South African Jacques Kallis who, on a flight to the subcontinent, looked out of the plane window hoping to
find the line that marks the equator and, when he was
running along a beach in Sri Lanka, asked one of his
team-mates where sea level was. And he is not like
Keith Miller who once flew across Germany, dodging
enemy fighters, just to get a close look at Bonn, the
birthplace of Beethoven, his hero. Warne's idea of culture is *Melrose Place* or *Happy Days*. He is seldom
introspective and is only so when he is forced to look
inside the shadowy depths of his personality because of
some scandal or controversy. Even then his insights on
himself and the world are unoriginal and vapid. God is
'the Bloke Upstairs' and life's changes are because the
Bloke Upstairs has deemed it to be, so there is no need

to venture into the meaning of what He has ordained for you. As for politics, he shows no interest and that is in keeping with most cricketers who are an innately conservative bunch and as such reflect the conservative nature of cricket, which is a game that reinforces tradition and old-fashioned values. And it's no bad thing that cricketers aren't interested in politics if one looks at the example of Imran Khan whose daydream it is to become Prime Minister of Pakistan. Judging by a recent documentary he made called *Imran Khan: Islam and America*, which was filled with *non sequiturs* and jaw-droppingly superficial political and religious insights, the ex-playboy, celebrity and cricketer would be well off putting aside any political ambitions forever.

Warne is a man who has found that inside the circumference of a cricket oval is a green Eden, in the centre of which is a turf strip of a stage where he can perform and master his own fate and find perfection, unlike outside its boundary fence, where he has found constant imperfection of which he has either been the cause or the hapless victim. This is not to disparage him. It is to point out that unfortunately for him he carries a symbolic load and a weight of expectations often outside his understanding or ken. The media, especially the press, seem to expect Warne to be more than he is and frequently find him wanting morally and culturally. He is mocked for his diet, his confession of never having read a book, for his indiscretions, his boofhead behaviour and statements, and castigated when he can't seem to grasp the importance of the mistakes he has made, as if he should in some way publicly flagellate himself. At times one wants to say to reporters and commentators, to quote from *The Life of Brian*, that Warne is not the Messiah, he's just a very naughty boy.

At the beginning of his Test career he probably never gave a thought to how important and successful he would become. His first captain, Allan Border, an astute judge of him, wrote: 'I'm sure Warney has achieved more than he ever thought he would. In some ways I think he still wonders how he ended up a great cricketer ... Not even he expected to make the impact on the game that he has and I'm sure there are times when he wonders how he arrived where he is now. Although there is still a little of the knockabout kid left in him, Warney has changed over the years. Anyone would with all the success and the fame it has brought. He is more guarded about people now, wary of who he lets get close to him and he's more savvy about his image. When he goes out now he's more aware of the attention whereas in his earlier days he was just a fun-loving bloke like thousands his age. The whole process has taken its toll but I think he is still the good solid bloke that he was at the start.'

In summing up his present life, team-mates frequently resort to the image of Warne as 'the Boy in the Bubble' or 'living his life in a fishbowl'. The intense media scrutiny is constant and pervasive. In Australian cricket some people compare Warne's renown to that of Dennis Lillee but the fast bowler's fame was nowhere near as widespread, due to the fact that television coverage of his deeds was pathetically limited compared to the ubiquitous worldwide media coverage of today. Lillee was never a celebrity like Warne and wouldn't have much liked it, but Warne does, even though he finds himself in the paradoxical position of being both a victim of it and a beneficiary. Like most celebrities, he gravitates towards other celebrities. His friendship with West Indian cricketer Brian Lara was based on their mutual love of being celebrities. Warne is thrilled that this power can gain him access to the best seats at a U2 concert and help him meet famous racing drivers and Kylie Minogue. On the walls of his den at home he proudly has pictures of himself meeting other celebrities such as basketballers Michael Jordan and Shaquille O'Neal and film star Sylvester Stallone.

Fame, and its oafish sidekick celebrity, are dangerous things. As Greg Chappell has remarked: 'Cricket is a tough game and if the players buy too much into the glamour and fame they don't survive. They make the mistake of thinking this is the real world and it's not. It's fantasyland.' For Errol Alcott, who has watched many a cricketer succumb to it, there is also a bleak side-effect: 'The media builds them up. The journalists give them a label. For instance, the media has given Steve Waugh the image of being a cool guy. Now that image might appeal to him and he will become that image. He has to some extent. No-one is really that cool … As a result, the way they perceive themselves and the way they know them-selves can be very different. A psychologist would have a field day with these guys.' But not necessarily with Warne. For despite all his fame and notoriety he is con-sidered by his team-mates to be remarkably grounded. He is content to see himself as just one of the boys, but in a way he was more prepared than fellow players to be

in the spotlight. From his boyhood years he has liked
to portray himself as a glamour boy. Just look at the
nicknames that have been bestowed on him by his
team-mates and journalists over the years – Hollywood,
Suicide Blonde, The Sultan of Swing or the Elvis Pres-
ley of Cricket. He likes the spotlight, he likes to be
adored and he knows that he is part of the entertainment industry. He has heard his name so often and has
become so used to his own image being reflected back
to him that, like Viv Richards, he has taken to speaking
of himself in the third person. Although criticised he
knows that he can sell his fame, but this is part of a commercial tradition that Richie Benaud fostered when, in
his playing days during the 1950s and 1960s, he sponsored everything from lawn mowers to hair creams.
Even the underside of fame and celebrity, when he felt
as if he were wilting in the withering glare of spotlights
that magnified his tiniest flaws, doesn't seem to have
affected him much once he stepped onto the cricket
field. When the English batsman Grahame Thorpe
found himself under tremendous strain after tabloids
reported allegations of an extramarital fling on an overseas tour, his cricket suffered and he looked increasingly
troubled. Left-arm spinner Phil Tufnell's public indiscretions (booze, girls, violence, domestic disturbances,
illegal substances, courtrooms and police cells) affected
his cricket and finally landed him in a psychiatric unit.
By contrast, when Warne is playing cricket, incidents off
the field vanish into a cosily hazy distance. He has the
optimistic disposition of an entrepreneur like Alan
Bond, whose wife was amazed that even in times of

great financial crisis he would sleep like a baby and wake up, as Warne says he does, 'with a smile on his dial'.

Yet for all his celebrity, fame and world travel, he has never really broadened his horizons. His fellow leg spinner Stuart MacGill is a man of the world. Warne likes junk food, MacGill fine dining, Warne likes beer and an occasional Midori with lemonade, MacGill is a wine buff, Warne has never read a book, MacGill likes reading and has earned captain Steve Waugh's wrath by reading when he should be watching his side play. Warne is gregarious and cannot stand to be alone, while there is the touch of the loner about MacGill who, when he travels, likes to experience the local culture. Warne is totally uninterested in other cultures. In his autobiography he really provides no impressions of India except for meeting Tendulkar at his home. His captain Steve Waugh has been determined to learn more about other societies and even helps fund a home for child lepers in India. Warne travels the world with blinkers on. In the subcontinent and South Africa he stays in five-star hotels or gated resorts like Sun City and ventures out only to play golf or gamble at a casino. Yet this is not an unusual attitude for cricketers. Allan Border was notorious for being uninterested in countries he toured. He couldn't even be bothered looking out the window to see the Taj Mahal.

Warne lives in a very different environment from former Australian players who had to put up with awful conditions when touring the subcontinent. Brian Booth remembers the 1964 tour where 'Everyone had diarrhoea. Norm [O'Neill] was crook, Johnny Martin had sunstroke, the cockroaches were running across the floor, the mattresses were a couple of inches thick and you couldn't sleep. And we just started laughing at the hopelessness of it, couldn't stop, laughed until we were almost sick.' The food was appalling and for some of the cricketers it seemed like they were 'prisoners of war'. Ian Meckiff could not get over the extremes of poverty and wealth and believed that he learnt more about life in the three months he spent there than all the rest of his days. Tom Veivers travelled to the subcontinent and South Africa and found that the poverty in India and the loathsome evil of apartheid transformed his view of the world and made him go on to become a politician.

All these reactions would be foreign to Warne because when touring he lives in a tightly circumscribed world of plush five-star hotels, room service, airplanes, cable television, croupiers, waiters, buses with videos and endless card games, security guards keeping away the *hoi polloi*, the humidicrib comfort of the dressing-room and the performing oval space of grass and pitch that is in itself also tightly circumscribed. He sees the world through the transparent or translucent glass of cars, buses and planes. The closest he gets to the rainbow nation of South Africa is bowling to a black opponent and the closest he gets to the masses on the subcontinent is peering uninterestedly at the waving brown hands and smiling teeth outside the team bus or signing autographs in the foyer of a grand hotel. He is a man who has little if any curiosity about the world. His world was determined years before as a Melbourne bayside teenager and he still lives in the area. In some respects he is like a rock-and-roller who found fame in his youth and has been content to be mollycoddled and stroked and enjoys a world that consists of self-reflecting images of himself. But unlike a rock-and-roller Warne's ego has been controlled by his own desire to be one of the boys and to conform to the grand Australian tradition of mateship.

Increasingly he has become haunted by the realisation that his future in the game is measured not so much in decades but in years, and a limited number of them at that. It must also be remembered that he has managed to maintain a reasonable equilibrium in the face of fame and celebrity because of the steady influence of his parents, to whom he has remained close – often listening to and taking their advice – his marriage to Simone, and their three children, Jackson, Brooke and Summer. Domesticity is his significant refuge. He has also learnt to laugh at himself. The mocking of his weight and his taste in food doesn't affect him as much anymore. He can make a fool of himself posing in front of a huge plate of baked beans in order to help a charity. But he can still be brittle at the abuse he receives. In late 2001 he clashed with a rigger at the Adelaide Cricket Ground who called him a 'poofter' and he angrily challenged the worker to repeat the comment. The public altercation only confirmed for a facetious reporter that 'Warne once described his life as like a soap opera. We agree. The only difficulty is trying to keep count on the number of episodes.'

Although he has changed, those closest to him see him as Border does: 'Unlike his bowling, Warney as a bloke is entirely straightforward. He lives life at breakneck pace and he can charm anyone. Whether he's talking to James Packer or the battler bloke in the pub, he's exactly the same guy. There's a public perception that he's a bit of a bighead, a lair, and he certainly is a confident and exuberant character. But he's an open book. He wears his heart on his sleeve.' He is still living his boyhood dream even now he is in his thirties. He is still boyishly enthusiastic about cricket. He literally gurgles with pleasure before a Test match is about to begin and can barely contain his excitement. In a way he hasn't grown up. Notice how reporters call him 'a big kid' or his fellow players speak of him as a 'knockabout kid' or 'the Boy in the Bubble'. He is still playing the game he played as a boy. Off the cricket paddock he has to be an adult but on it he can still be a child. He is Peter Pan, the cricket field is his Never Land and the applause of the spectators makes him invincible.

He has achieved nearly everything he desired in cricket except for the captaincy. He was named one of the five *Wisden* cricketers of the twentieth century, along with Sir Donald Bradman, Sir Garfield Sobers, Sir Vivian Richards and Sir Jack Hobbs (although he ruefully recognises that, given his many misdemeanours, even if Australia still had knighthoods he would surely be the only unknighted cricketer in the list). At present he is the second-greatest wicket taker in history. It is probable that the off spinner Muttiah Muralitharan will soon pass him, but the Sri Lankan's records will always be sullied by the fact that he chucks or throws the ball and has been called by umpires for bowling illegal deliveries. When Warne retires he will find the wrench of not playing extremely testing. He will miss the fame and the game of course, but also the camaraderie of fellow players and mateship, which he values so highly. He will miss the refuge of the dressing-room with its banter, silly practical jokes, the smell of sweat, leather, linament, the 'coffins' over-spilling with cricket gear and the skylarking, celebratory beers after a long, hot day in the field and singing the team song after a victory. He will miss the noise and excitement of one-day games, a din so loud that players on the field can only compare it to a rock concert. That's why he will stay connected to sport and especially cricket. Like his hero Michael Jordan he will invest in restaurants and sports management – and has already made plans to do so, having incorporated his name. He predicts a range of enterprises which he believes will be 'something pretty big' and he sees himself as playing chief executive roles. Television has been grooming him for a decade now and he will try commentating. He has a pleasant voice, unlike his former captain Mark Taylor, whose voice sounds like he is gargling marbles. His few forays into commentating have proved that he is intelligent, knowing and shrewd about the game.

He can retire with great satisfaction because he knows he has achieved much. He has brought back the crowds, made cricket again a game of skill, cunning and variety unlike the brutal monotony of past decades. He has thrilled cricket lovers across the globe and has awed both spectators and batsmen with the skills of a magician. Every time he has come up to bowl it is as if the game has been transported into a heightened state of expectation and audacity. He has changed the 'narrative' of the televising of Test cricket. And, yes, he has provided a sport with a satisfaction and beauty that is closer to the moves of a chess master or the aesthetics of an artist than that of a mere cricketer. Even on the debit side his personal scandals and controversies have made cricketers less dull. He has become the first true cricket celebrity. Perhaps it is the former great bowler Dennis Lillee who has summed up Warne's appeal better than anyone else: 'He is the only guy I've watched since I retired to cause the hair to stand up on the back of my neck.'

The End

Appendix

Throughout this book I have called Warne a champion but a definition of what constitutes a champion is elusive. Rudi Webster, author of *Winning Ways*, says: 'When you're dealing with a champion you never have him beaten until he is flat on his back.' In the recent book *What Makes A Champion!* the editor, Allan Snyder of the Australian National University, argues that a champion in sport or elsewhere has a particular mind-set, a particular way of viewing things. 'This champion mind-set,' he says, 'is often characterised by an aversion to being average: champions don't necessarily want to be better than others but they do want to be different, which often shows up early in life in an independent, unconventional, even rebellious streak.' People with such a mind-set have a capacity for fighting adversity, he adds, learning and benefiting from each failure as they go. These comments ring true for Warne, as do several others by contributors to the book. Neuropsychologist Professor Elkhonon Goldberg believes that: 'A champion, a winner, a leader is able to focus on a goal, no matter how distant it may be, and to dedicate all his or her resources to that goal without allowing these resources to be diluted by trivialities.' John Eales, former Australian rugby captain, cites family environment as a key factor, which in Warne's youth was vitally important as both parents supported him totally in his wish to become a sportsman. What is also interesting is how several champions were not that impressive in their youths. Norm O'Neill, a former Test player, once stated that when he was at high school there were several cricketers better than he but he went on because he developed a single-mindedness and, although he didn't state it, a mental toughness. Champions like Warne also have a positive outlook. They refuse to think negative thoughts, they refuse to give in or contemplate defeat. Instinctively a champion knows that thoughts and emotions affect the performance. Negative emotions badly affect the heart rate, whereas positive ones help the body to recover. Also a positive outlook in Warne's case always leads him to believe that a wicket will soon fall and that it is the batsman that will make the mistake, not him. Over his decade in cricket he discovered something that the West Indian champion Gary Sobers had also learnt: 'Perhaps more than anything else you have to know your strengths and weaknesses.' This may seem a cliché but it is one of the hardest lessons of all to master, especially during periods of great pressure when the temptation is to experiment out of a sense of exasperation rather than strategy.

It is Australian coach John Buchanan who gives the

most vivid example of Warne's positive temperament. During the vital Third Test against India in 2001 Australia was in trouble. 'It was the third or fourth day and India were well on top. Everyone was having a hard time, and Warney was pretty down,' said Buchanan of Australia's key bowler who had a dismal 10 wickets for 50 runs in the series, 'but at lunch and tea times he just stood up and really excited everybody by his own enthusiasm, willing everybody to win. He just stood head and shoulders above everybody at that point, just with his desire to lift not only himself but everybody else around him. This was one last chance of beating India, and he didn't want it to slip away … He, like anybody, could have easily huddled in a corner and said: "Oh, well, we'll give it our best shot." But he wasn't going to be beaten, and that's part of the reason he's where he is.'

Bibliography

Birley, Derek *The Willow Myth: Some Cricket Myths Explored*
(2000). London: Aurum Press.

Border, Allan; Langer, Justin; Warne, Shane; Waugh, Steve
The Dominators (2000). Sydney: Hodder

Buzo, Alex *Glancing Blows* (1987). Ringwood, Victoria:
Penguin Books

Cashman, Richard *et al* (ed.) *The Oxford Companion to
Australian Cricket* (1996). Melbourne: Oxford University
Press

Coward, Mike *Cricket Beyond The Bazaar* (1990). Sydney:
Allen & Unwin

Edmonds, Frances *Another Bloody Tour* (1986). London: William
Heinemann

Fishman, Roland *Calypso Cricket* (1991). McMahons Point,
NSW: Margaret Gee Publishing

Frith, David *Silence of the Heart: Cricket Suicides* (2001).
London: Mainstream Publishing

Gately, Mark *Waugh Declared* (1992). Sydney: Ironbark Press

Haigh, Gideon (ed.) *Australian Cricket Anecdotes* (1996). South
Melbourne, Victoria: Oxford University Press

Haigh,Gideon *The Summer Game* (1997). Melbourne:Text
    Publishing
Healy, Ian *The Autobiography* (2000). Sydney: Harper Collins
Harms, John *Confessions of a Thirteenth Man* (1999).
    Melbourne:Text Publishing
Hopps, David *We're Right Behind You, Captain!* (1997). London:
    Robson Books
Jenner,Terry with Ken Piesse *T.J. Over the Top* (2000).
    Melbourne: Information Australia
Keane, Patrick *Merv:The Full Story* (1997). Sydney: Harper
    Collins
Knox, Malcom *Taylor & Beyond* (2000). Sydney:ABC Books
McHarg, Jack *Bill O'Reilly:A Cricketing Life* (1990). Sydney:
    Millennium Books
Magazine, Pradeep *Not Quite Cricket* (1999). New Delhi:
    Penguin Books
Mallet,Ashley *Clarrie Grimmett:The Bradman of Spin* (1993).
    St. Lucia: University of Queensland Press
Marquesee, Mike *War Minus the Shooting* (1996). London:
    William Heinemann
Martin-Jenkins, Christopher and de Lisle, Charles
    An Australian Summer (1999). London: Faber and Faber
Perry, Roland *Bold Warnie* (1999). Sydney: Random House
Piesse, Ken *The Complete Shane Warne* (1999). Ringwood,
    Victoria: Penguin Books
Piesse, Ken *Cricket's Greatest Scandals* (2000). Ringwood,
    Victoria: Penguin Books
Pollard, Jack *The World's Greatest Leg Spinners* (1994).
    Kenthurst, NSW: Kangaroo Press
Rae, Simon *It's Not Cricket* (2001). London: Faber and Faber
Roussel, Raymond *Comment j'ai ecrit certain des mes livres*
    (1935). Paris: Lemerre
Taylor, Mark *A Captain's Year* (1997) Sydney: Pan Macmillan

Warne, Shane with Richard Hobson *Shane Warne: My Autobiography* (2001). London: Hodder & Stoughton

Waugh, Mark with Grantlee Keiza *A Year To Remember* (1997). Sydney: Random House

Waugh, Steve *No Regrets* (1999). Sydney: Harper Collins

Waugh, Steve *Ashes Diary 2001* (2001). Sydney: Harper Collins

Wilkins, Brian *Cricket: The Bowler's Art* (1997). East Roseville, NSW: Kangaroo Press

Winder, Robert *Hell For Leather* (1996). London: Victor Gollancz

Notes

Page 8
As related in Viola Tait's *Dames, Principal Boys … and All That* the
highlight of the show was the 'March of Juvenile Cricketers' which
consisted of 'eleven small boys dressed in cricket whites and carrying
bats. The captain of the team was dressed to resemble W.G.Grace,
sporting a big black beard and drooping moustache.' The Australian
team was represented by the 'Ladies of the Ballet' who made their
entrance singing 'Cricketing Song' to the tune of the 'Gens d'armes'
Duet' from *Genevieve de Brabant*.

Page 8
Pinter and Stoppard played in the same team for years. Pinter was a
very competent batsman and Stoppard a wicket-keeper.

Page 16
His love of speed was confirmed when he was banned for three
months after breaking the speed limit in England. His late-model
cars have also been the victims of that particular Australian sign of
envy – deliberate scratching of the duco.

Page 29
I suppose it's logical that a poet would compare himself to a cricketer,
but as John Willet, the translator of Brecht, once said to me: 'All poets
are shits.' Having met many poets over the years I have never had
cause to question that judgement.

Page 41
The English mistakenly call Warne a surfer. The bayside beaches
provide nothing like the rampaging surf of the NSW coastline, but
the label is in keeping with the average Briton's knowledge of
Australia, gained from *Neighbours* and images of Bondi Beach.

Page 43
Even in 2002 Warne still harbours dreams of playing football. Fitter
than he has been for over a decade, the 32-year-old told the press that
he'd like to 'play a year of football before I get too old'

Page 55
Even during the match the Australian physiotherapist Errol Alcott had
to stop Warne from scoffing down party pies during the game breaks.

Page 60
One of Jenner's suggestions that especially pinned itself to the message
board of Warne's mind was what to do when a batsman comes in at
the non-striker's end: 'I'll immediately bowl a big wrong'un. It doesn't
matter if the batsman facing picks it. You're bowling it for the benefit
of the non-striker and the other guys sitting in the shed so they can
see that the ball is spinning. When it's their turn to face, he's looking
for the wrong'un so you starve him of it.' It was advice that was to
bring Warne great successes.

Page 123
Waugh also has a deep and abiding interest in trotting and has bought
several horses, even though he is allergic to horse hair.

Page 157
Her voice had that inimitable contemporary English accent that places
consonants and vowels sounds in a heavy blender of a lazy tongue and
they emerge as an impenetrable gargle that makes even a bad Australian pronunciation sound like the Queen's English.

Page 159
There was an interesting follow-up to this. The disgraced footballer,
Wayne Carey, fled Melbourne and the best friend, Anthony Stevens,
the man whom he betrayed, was made captain of the North

Melbourne club. Opposition players were asked by the press if they would 'sledge' Stevens about the affair during a game. All said no. Warne was asked and said that he would consider doing so. The press reaction was predictable: during the next couple of days sports journalists went after Warne with their usual pontificating nonsense.

Page 169
The microphone only picked up Inzamam calling in Urdu for two runs (which would have been four runs for a more athletic team-mate).

Page 174
Average Australian run-rates before 2000 were 2.75 but they're now up near four runs an over.

Page 175
Occasionally when Warne feels under siege in Australia he threatens to go and live in England after retirement, saying in late 2001, 'Sometimes in Australia they look for the negatives, the bad things. Over in England it's a bit more positive.'

Page 191
There is a stubborn myth that Bradman disliked the Australian/Irish Catholic members of his team, especially Bill O'Reilly. In reality Bradman was a fastidious man who disliked the culture of the bar and boozing which is an integral part of Australian/Irish culture.

Page 199
Even as I write there are articles in the newspapers bemoaning the fact that although Asian-Australian students are brilliant they don't become a part of the ethos of Australian schools: they do not play sport.

Page 206
At the 1996 World Cup Warne gave a bizarre and limp explanation as to why the Australian team didn't play in Colombo. He said the issue was not about cricket, it was just that it wouldn't be safe to go shopping. The irritated Sri Lankan foreign minister, Lakshman Kadirgamar, retorted 'shopping is for sissies'.

Page 234
Even Bishen Bedi, the former great Indian spin bowler, is convinced
the Sri Lankan is a chucker. Adam Gilchrist said in May, 2002 that the
trouble with Muttiah Muralitharan's success is that Sri Lankan boys
are copying his dubious action.

Also available from Duffy & Snellgrove

The Seven Rivers
Douglas Stewart

'What is the most harrowing way in which you can lose a trout? One that caused me quite exceptional agony was a fish that simply rose once to look at bait and then was seen no more. It was in the Tangatara one golden morning; and it was the hugest fish that ever I lost. It was so big that I don't even believe in it myself'

First published in 1966, Douglas Stewart's book is still considered the classic account of fly-fishing in Australia and New Zealand. To the stories of fishing, from Lake Taupo to the Snowy River, Stewart brings his poet's eye for nature and for the human beings encountered along the way. Fishing, as he makes clear with his sense of humour and drama, is about much more than fish.

ISBN 1 875989 99 4

Also available from Duffy & Snellgrove

Mungo: the man who laughs
Mungo MacCallum

When Mungo MacCallum moved
to Canberra in 1967, he was imm-
mediatey caught up in the maelstrom of politcal activity
which was sweeping Australia. He became one of the
most influential and wittiest political chroniclers of the
Whitlam period, writing consistently entertaining
material about the political animals who inhabit Parlia-
ment House.

This book follows his political education, from an ado-
lescent watching Prime Minister Evatt sticking potato
chips in his hair to the Whitlam victory of 1972. It
charts the events and people who shaped our history
and looks at the factors that led to this unprecedented
time in Australia's political life.

ISBN 1 876631 50 3

Also available from Duffy & Snellgrove

The Wooden Leg of
Inspector Anders
Marshall Browne

This first book in the Inspector Anders series won the Ned Kelly Award, and has been published in the UK, the USA and is currently being translated for publication in Europe.

Inspector Anders is sent to a city in southern Italy to investigate the killing of a respected judge. There he finds himself drawn into a shadowy world of corruption and power, and becomes increasingly involved with both the case and the judge's widow. Once Anders was a hero. Then he lost his leg – and his nerve – to an anarchist bomb. Now the widow is offering him the chance to redeem his life with one last explosive act of courage.

ISBN 1 876631 15 5